AUTO SALES

HOW TO EXCEL IN THE CAREER OF SELLING CARS

JB Zegalia

Llumina
Press

AUTO SALES

HOW TO EXCEL IN THE CAREER OF SELLING CARS

autosalesbook.com

ISBN: 978-1-62550-499-9

TABLE OF CONTENTS

INTRODUCTION   i

THE SALES PROCESS

1   GREETING AND RAPPORT   1

2   SELECT A VEHICLE   13

3   PRESENT THE VEHICLE   29

4   APPRAISE THE TRADE   41

5   BUILD VALUE   47

6   PREPARE FOR THE NEGOTIATION   53

7   PRESENT THE FIGURES   63

8   CLOSE THE SALE   75

9   MY FAVORITE CLOSES   91

10   OVERCOME OBJECTIONS   105

11   STILL CLOSING   123

THE ESSENTIALS

12   LET ME ASK YOU A QUESTION   129

13   READING PEOPLE   143

UNDERSTANDING OUR CUSTOMERS

14   WHY A CUSTOMER BUYS   153

15   RECOGNIZE THE SIGNS   167

16   BUYING PERSONALITIES   177

Understanding Ourselves

17 TRAITS OF A TOP SALESPERSON   193

18 QUESTIONS ANSWERED   205

Supporting Knowledge

19 THE TELEPHONE   213

20 LISTENING   233

21 PROSPECTING   243

22 THE INTERNET   249

23 KEEPING YOUR FOCUS   261

INTRODUCTION

A career in sales is more than just a job; it is like being the director of your own company. It gives you the unlimited potential to succeed and the ability to do it at any stage in your work history. It is a career where you are not limited to a set goal or range of income. It is also a career where your ability to learn and your desire for knowledge are the keys to your production.

There are basic steps in selling a car, each of which builds off the preceding one toward the completion of the sale. In this book, each chapter will outline the goal of each step and give you real world advice on what to do and how to do it. This book will take you through the steps of the sales process that will smoothly transition your customers from introduction to delivery.

There is a reason certain salespeople will consistently outperform others in our business. Some will choose to learn their trade and some will not. The most encouraging fact is that sales is also a business where anyone with the desire to learn can achieve the level of success that he or she will choose. Skill and knowledge are qualities that can be learned and forever improved upon with your desire to be successful.

This book was written for just such a salesperson. It was designed to help you understand each step of the sale and give you a comprehensive guide to follow. With this book you will learn how to set up your business, build rapport, and gain credibility. You will learn to be inquisitive, persuasive, develop relationships, handle objections, and ultimately, make the sale. Soon, you will be one of your dealership's top sellers. Let's get started.

GREETING AND RAPPORT

The greeting and rapport stage is one of the most important steps in the sales process. It sets the stage on which all other steps are set. Your goal here is to welcome your customers and create an atmosphere in which they will be comfortable. When a customer walks in your door, you want to set your focus and let the show begin.

THE GREETING

Have you ever walked into a store where you felt the salesperson just wouldn't leave you alone? Has a salesperson ever just seemed to force him or herself on you without your acceptance?

At this early stage, it is essential that you are able to provide your customers with an immediate feeling of comfort. Learn to welcome them with your eyes and your expression. Develop a sincere smile and an open manner.

In sales, your greeting will always be more successful if you are able to invite your customers to initiate the greeting instead of forcing one upon them. Do not make your customers feel as though they have to talk to you. Present them with a greeting that they want to respond to in a positive way.

OBSERVE AND ADAPT

In the first stage of your introduction, it is usually a good idea to allow your customers some space. Engage them slowly and try to determine their initial level of outgoingness. When you see an uneasy or defensive customer, take it slow, giving them the time to settle and feel more at ease. If your customer appears to be more confident and outgoing, simply adjust your approach to match theirs. Always greet your customers with similar actions.

When greeting a new customer, keep in mind that all but the most outgoing will have some degree of anxiety. Know that you must slowly work to diffuse this before you can build in to the rapport stage. Watch their movements and expressions. Listen to their tone of voice.

A shy person may look down, face away, and speak softly. An outgoing person will look you in the eye, face directly, and speak with confidence. To best excel at this stage, you want to be able to analyze your customers quickly and proceed accordingly. Seek to adjust your greeting to match their initial level of outgoingness and personality. Practice several different approaches for your greetings, adjusting them to best create a comfortable atmosphere for each of the people you meet.

COMFORT AND STYLE

Picture the difference in atmosphere between a local barbeque and an uptown restaurant. Think of the unique interactions involving the people attending. Is it safe to say that certain people will feel more comfortable in one place than the other?

People like to interact in a manner of their liking so your greeting should always be adjusted to fit the preferred style of your customer.

You must provide an atmosphere that is comfortable to them in order to gain the interest needed to interact. Analyze their actions and mannerisms to get a feel for their preferred approach. Become aware of your customer's personal and emotional presence and establish the best approach for each.

ENAGAGE YOUR CUSTOMERS

When first greeting a customer, take notice of what may stand out, comment positively, and ask your question. Start with an opening that will invite a conversation, not one that will produce a defensive response. If you can, try to cater a question specific to each individual.

Your opening may be, "A Cowboys fan, I see," while noticing their hat or jacket, or, "So how often do you get to go biking?" while noticing their bike rack. A question that will start a conversation and avoid a defensive response will always promote a good start. The type of question to ask here is an open-ended question. This will allow your customers to expand their answers however they want. It will invite conversation and help create the flow of your communication.

I like these types of introductions because they do not involve a yes or no answer. They are question based and will invite your newly greeted customers involvement. Your customers will always be more likely to respond in a positive manner if you encourage a comfortable interaction before bringing up the business at hand.

There are many similar openings that will engage your customers. Come up with a style that you will feel comfortable in using. Look to prepare for the people you will soon greet. Once you have successfully observed and matched their outgoingness, initiated a pleasant greeting and engaged them, you'll be better able to adjust and adapt as you interact.

EYE CONTACT

For all greetings, make sure you maintain good eye contact with your customers. Try to produce a welcoming look of trust and understanding while looking into their eyes. Avoid the temptation to look down or away when speaking. Remember, what you say with your eyes will be believed, what you say while looking away will be questioned.

Your goal here is to create a sense of confidence and honesty, and a warm smile and good eye contact is always your best approach.

To help further your effectiveness in your greetings, try to visualize how others see you. When you are able to see yourself in an objective manner, you will better understand how others will see and feel about you.

USE YOUR CUSTOMER'S NAMES

I heard somewhere that the sweetest sound to someone's ears is his or her own name. I couldn't agree more. Learn your customer's name early in your meeting and use it during the course of your conversation. If a customer has a difficult name, practice the correct pronunciation with him or her. This will show that you care and help avoid future embarrassment.

However, always use their name casually and in a normal tone. Try to refer to customers by name when you are in a light topic or a non-business conversation. If your customers feel you are using a technique they will be less likely to trust you, and people have a keen sense for when you are being insincere. Fortunately, the more you practice this, the more sincere you will become.

MIRRORING YOUR CUSTOMERS

Have you ever gone somewhere, like to a different part of the country, and come back with an accent? If you did, you were mirroring. You were subconsciously fitting in by adjusting your manner and style. Mirroring is a safe and effective way to further your rapport. After you have successfully engaged your customers to open up, you want to continue building a comfortable environment.

To help accomplish this, slowly transform your speech, mannerisms, and actions to mirror theirs. If they walk slowly, walk slowly. If they are outgoing and humorous, be outgoing and humorous.

4

If they are quick and businesslike, answer directly and act professionally. Your customers will always feel more at ease if they feel they are with someone who is like them. As long as you are careful not to overdo or exaggerate your efforts, this is a valuable tool to help you establish rapport.

Take the time to learn some of the terms and phrases of the more common professions and activities in the area where you sell. Become knowledgeable in outside topics such as work, school, sports, local news, and even recent events to help establish a basis for common-ground topics and preferred language. When talking to an engineer, be informative. When talking to a business man, be professional. When talking to a carpenter dressed in a T-shirt, put your foot on a truck bumper and say, "How 'bout this one?" Just kidding, but you get the idea. Place yourself in the best position to communicate by providing a comfort for your customers. It is usually in the early stages of their visit that they will predetermine how long they stay.

SHAKING HANDS

I think there is a time and place to shake a customer's hand. Two such occasions may be when you are welcoming them back to your dealership and a rapport has already been established, and possibly, when you and your customers have agreed upon a deal. Note that in both of these situations you have had ample time to understand your customer's style while interacting.

For your first meeting however, in a sales setting, I feel you should not always be the first to extend your hand. Understand that many customers may be uncomfortable being approached in this manner at this early stage. Your customers may feel you are invading their space. Every customer you greet will have his or her own comfort zone, and entering it too soon may increase his or her level of anxiety.

I understand different people may have differing opinions on this topic, and I was even a little hesitant to include it; however, I do feel strongly that this is a perspective you may want to consider. Old influences are sometimes taken for granted and are hard to understand; however, think back to past introductions or watch others in the future. A majority of the time, you will notice the lack of ease surrounding the handshake in the first introduction. Well, you can eliminate this uneasiness if you do not force customers to shake. While researching this belief, I found that most customers agreed with this line of thinking while most salespeople did not. I think this is because the salespeople were thinking about their early training, where the customers were thinking objectively about their point of view.

Skillful salespeople will always seek to be invited in, not to invite themselves in. To be safe, seek to measure your customer's willingness to interact before you offer to shake. If they are outgoing and positive, it may be okay. However, if they're shy and reserved, it may be a mistake. When you approach your customers, know that you will still have ample opportunity to respond if you misjudged their willingness and they initiate a handshake. You should be able to see your customer's hands rise, even while looking into their eyes. Nevertheless, you should always welcome your customers with a warm smile and an open manner, not with an awkward handshake.

ALL ABOUT THE RAPPORT

A proper greeting sets the foundation for your customer's acceptance of you. It allows you to create the interest and attention that will better promote a sale. Once your customers start to see you as a likable person they will be more likely to offer you their time. This will afford you the opportunity to further understand and better adapt to the people you are working with, all while helping you keep them willing to proceed. Establishing a rapport accomplishes two effects; it distracts them from their anxiety and lets you create yourself as a person who is on their level. This is critical down the road. A person is always more easily persuaded by a peer than an outsider.

The first step in building rapport is to find the common ground needed to initiate and carry on a conversation. The goal here is to have your prospective customers open up and share an experience or common interest with you.

The whole time the greeting is taking place, you should be busy observing your opportunities. You should be scanning and developing the clues on how to create the common ground needed to build your rapport. The clues that will help form your common ground are always present if you are observant. They may be in the accessories on the vehicle your customers drove up in, like a college window sticker or a parking pass for their work, or in the clothing they wear, such as a uniform or a sports name on a hat.

The idea here is to take them visually to a place they enjoy. Different manufacturers and areas of town may have diverse customers, but your dealership is stationary and your product is unique, so there will be plenty of area specific topics of conversation. Familiarize yourself with the typical interests that customers who walk in your door may have. Learn the local flavor and develop some topics of conversation. Every area and person has an interest that can be determined through your efforts. It might be camping, baseball, traveling, or even their kids. Take these examples and visualize how they can be used to invite a conversation. If you're able to share a small point or mutual opinion on a topic of their interest, customers will be more likely to open up and share a story about their interests with you. And if they do, you have established rapport.

If you have no clues, ask some light questions as you interact to help get your customer's started. Vary your directness with their response. Some examples may be: What do you do for a living, how far was your ride in today, or, what do you do when you're not working?

Engage your customers. Have them open up with their individual likes. Inquire about their hopes, dreams, and favorite places for vacation. Use their answers as a tool to help alleviate the early anxieties that may be present and allow a less inhibited path to discovering their needs.

In this stage, you must be able to portray a friendly, open attitude and pay attention to what the customer is saying and feeling. Skillful salespeople will always do more listening than talking. They will develop their conversation into an invitation to offer information. Once you start developing rapport, develop a balance of common interest and involvement questions to both stimulate a conversation and determine the wants and needs of your customers. Position yourself as someone your customers will like and want to do business with.

Know your path and your destination before you start each step. Visualize the process. Build one step at a time. Greet, develop rapport, question, demonstrate, develop desire, build value, handle objections, persuade, and close. Every single step of the sale will go more smoothly if you are able to establish a connection with your customers. People will prefer to spend time with and ultimately buy from you if they are able to connect with you. Do not skip this step or underestimate its importance. Understanding your customers and identifying with their emotions and unique preferences is how you are best able to meet and continue working with each as an individual. All top salespeople are aware of this and have become skilled in observation and understanding. They have learned the importance of working successfully with different styles and personalities.

CREATE A SENSE OF HUMOR

There is no quicker route to having people like you than making them laugh. Even the most guarded will open up with some humor. It is the mild distraction that will make them more receptive to your persuasion. A good sense of humor is also a great way to take the anxiety out of the sales process. It will take the edge off any situation.

My two favorite types of humor for sales, are clever humor and ridiculous humor. Know that in many cases, your goal is simply to lighten the tone of what may be an anxious setting. An example would be to say something clearly obvious while looking at your customers with a straight face. As they look back with curiosity, as if to say, "Are you serious?" give a little grin to let them know you are not.

They will smile, and you will have shared your first laugh.

Use your imagination and creativity to develop some humor and then become comfortable using it. Choose a presentation style that best fits your personality and the atmosphere you create when interacting. Think of past experiences where you and previous customers were able to share a laugh and recreate the experience for new ones. Remember, you will have a different audience every day, so you can continue with your most successful material every day.

Here are a couple of examples of my favorites:

- When a husband and wife are about to take a test drive, I will look with concern at one of them and ask him or her to, "keep an eye on the other," and then smile. Since I have just met both of them, it is fun to watch their reaction to the curious level of trust that I have for one of them.

- Before a test drive, I will ask with a straight face, "Do you want a dealer tag on the car you're test driving, or do you want to risk it?" And then I smile.

- With the hood of the car up, I will point and say with all the pride and seriousness in the world, "That's the engine right there." When my customers look over and grin, I follow up with, "Well, I just went to car-sales school, and sometimes I just like to show off." Break the ice. Loosen the tension. Have fun.

- If someone asks you the miles per gallon, look at them intently and ask, "Do you drive more uphill or downhill?" The key here is to look very serious and analytical. Then just when they think you're serious, give them your smile. Let them have fun. If you can make them laugh, you can sell them a car. Note that this type of humor can also be used as a gauge of their level of humor. It will tell you whether you have an emotional or a logical customer. Upon learning new information from their reactions, adjust your approach as necessary.

- If you're having a hard time getting your customers to come inside to work out a deal, smile and say, "Look, are you going to come in peacefully, or do I need to go get some help?" Then start to smile. This, of course, is for when you are in the proper character and while the interaction leading up to your request has already been one of light humor.

- Okay, this is my favorite. This will make just about anybody smile. While working a deal, ask your manager a question while speaking normally and in obvious hearing distance of your customers, like right in front of them. Start out with, "Look, I don't want my customers to hear me, but…" and then ask your question. Almost all of your customers will think this is funny, because it is so apparent that they can, in fact, hear you. It also gives you the opportunity to say something out loud and directed at them that you kind of don't have to take responsibility for, because you're making believe that they can't hear you. Get it?

With humor, know that it's often just as effective to mildly break away from the anxiety at hand as it is to have your customers falling over with laughter. If you're able to match a style of humor with a particular situation and lighten or avoid certain conditions, you can often aid the newly created atmosphere. Naturally, too much humor or the wrong style may not be advised, but if people are encouraged to see situations less seriously they may become pleasantly distracted and more easily persuaded. The next time you feel you have the right set of customers and they may appreciate a small break, a little humor may be the best remedy.

Okay, now try some that you like. Oh, and if you are not laughing now, maybe you should work on your delivery, because it's all in the delivery.

FINAL NOTE

The best way to interact with someone is always with a shared enthusiasm. Understand that the best way to lead a customer is to first connect with them. Every successful process will need a solid foundation. You will not be able to enlighten someone on what he or she should buy without first having them willing to listen. Your customer's decision will only follow the path of your recommendation if you are able to successfully open and attain their willingness to proceed.

The purpose of our greeting is to create a receptive customer. One who will find comfort in following the process you set. Observe, adapt and welcome your customer. As with any process, the best way to begin is by first preparing.

2

SELECT A VEHICLE

The next step in the sales process is to help our customers select the offering that will be right for them. When a customer walks in your door, most will have some idea of what they are looking for. It is your job to help them determine exactly what they're looking for and narrow their focus to one specific choice.

SET YOURSELF UP FOR SUCCESS

It is here, in this early stage of the process, that your presence will have its greatest impact. Be confident in yourself and your vehicles. Show concern for your customer's needs and respect for their style. Portray yourself as a person who wants to help find the right vehicle for them, not someone who just wants to make a sale. Help them determine the vehicle that would be best for them by the input you request and then help them realize it with the support of your influence.

Here, more than ever, is where you need to have established rapport and gained credibility. In other words, your opinion has to count. You have to be informed, likeable, and trustworthy. People want to learn and be educated as to the right car for them. Your customers are looking for a competent, informed professional to help them in the purchase of their new automobile. They want guidance. Know your line of vehicles and understand how their features match up to the benefits they are seeking.

DETERMINE THEIR MOTIVATION

The selection stage starts with a question. Ask yourself, "What event has occurred to bring them to my dealership?" Recognize the need or want that has precipitated their visit, then work to find the vehicle that will best satisfy them. Is their current vehicle in need of frequent repairs? Has a new job created the desire for a nicer car? Does a recent travel trailer purchase necessitate a larger towing capacity? Are they looking for safety, status, luxury, comfort, and rear seat room, or do they just want a car other than the green colored one they already have?

To help select your customer's best choice, it's essential to establish what's important to them. Do not just randomly start to demonstrate all the vehicles in your line. This will show that you do not care about their needs and only care about selling them anything. For example, it would be counterproductive to talk about a vehicle's power, when economy is what they're concerned with. However, without taking the time or effort to inquire into your customer's motivations before you start your demonstration, you would never know this.

When selecting, understand that certain features will motivate people differently. To some, having four-wheel drive may mean traction on the snow days and better resale value. To others, however, four-wheel drive may mean less fuel economy and a higher initial cost. Some will travel in snow country; some will not. A top salesperson will not demonstrate a particular vehicle or sell the benefits of a vehicle's features before they know what benefits are important to their customers.

Additional insight may be found in their previous vehicle. If they liked their old car and it just needs replacing, you might want to select a vehicle with similar features. If they want to improve on their previous vehicle, determine what features they are looking to add or change. Once you have determined what they are looking for, you

14

will be better equipped to persuade them by confirming the credible points of their selection.

INVOLVE THEIR EMOTIONS

The key in successfully completing this stage is to search out the vehicle that will not only satisfy your customer's needs, but will also excite them, the one vehicle that will best create the desire to want to own it today. Understand that the selection stage will always be better received, and sometimes only received, if you are able to help select a choice the customer will want to buy.

THE THREE COMMON PATHS OF SELECTION

There are three different situations that present themselves when a customer walks in your door. In the first, your customers will not have a set vehicle in mind. In the second, they will know what they want and you will have one in stock. In the third, they will know what they want, but you will not have their choice in stock.

Let's take a look.

1. IF THEY DO NOT HAVE A SET VEHICLE IN MIND; INVITE THEM TO YOUR INVENTORY

When the customers you are working with do not know the exact vehicle they're looking for, invite them back into your inventory. Many customers are visually oriented. Because these customers are visiting without knowing what they want, they will be likely to choose a vehicle based on how it appeals to them in person. These are the people who want more than to just look on the internet or read the consumer books. They want to see and touch the different vehicles available.

Since these customers don't know exactly what they want, you will often need to help them with the narrowing process. Start by

15

determining the basic type of vehicle they have in mind. This process is both started and finished with a series of investigative questions. Your further research for this stage can take place while you're walking in the direction of your inventory.

"Do you think you might be interested in a car or truck? Okay, a four-door or two-door? A compact or a midsize? A four-cylinder or a six-cylinder? A light color or a dark color?" And so on. Start with a wide scope and slowly narrow your focus using the parameters they give you. Your purpose here is to center in on a smaller set of choices. You will also gain credibility with your questions. Your customers will feel that you're better able to help guide them if you have the proper information to do so. Listen to their needs and understand what they're trying to accomplish. From here, continue the narrowing process by including vehicles that have features they like and eliminating others that are determined unacceptable.

NARROW WITH CAUTION

When initiating your questioning process, it is important to use a broad scope approach so you don't limit too much of your inventory early on. This way, there can still be an open group of vehicles while you continue to determine what features they consider necessary and which they consider optional. An example would be to ask if they are looking for a light color or dark color or if they would like their vehicle loaded or lightly equipped.

This will help narrow their selection yet still leave you with a range of vehicles that are acceptable. For example, you may not want to eliminate medium blue specifically just yet because that may be the only color you have in which their other desired features line up. What you are trying to avoid here is finding the perfect vehicle as it relates to most of their criteria, only to have already eliminated it earlier in the process.

16

While in this stage, it may also be good practice to test different combinations of your vehicle's options with your customer. This is to help anticipate future objections when searching for the right combination. When doing so, if you are able to foresee their most likely choice will not line up perfectly with your inventory, you may want to help influence them on the benefits of similar features of your in stock vehicles. As long as they are not compromising their needs by eliminating a specific requirement, offering them the opportunity to consider some alternatives may turn out in their favor. In addition to increasing the possibility of finding an acceptable vehicle, your customers may genuinely appreciate the benefits of additional features or qualities.

PREAPARE FOR THE UNEXPECTED

When making a selection, there will always be the unforeseen objections and obstacles that may occur. At any point in time, something can go off track and you may find yourself backing up, starting over, or unable to move forward. There will always be the hesitations and uncertainties to contend with. However, if you continue to move forward in an inquiring manner, you will often realize your next best move. To help in your selection, here is a look at a couple of the more common challenges you may face in this scenario and some advice for handling them.

SIMILAR CHOICES

One obstacle that may occur when making a selection is the decision process for closely related choices. For example, if they like both blue and burgundy or both sets of optional wheels, you will often have to help them focus on just one before you can move to the next step.

The key to resolving this is to investigate the preferences they have in each while slowly starting to focus in on their most likely choice. Meaning, present both sides of their preferences equally in the early stages of their decision, and then gradually lean your measure of influence to the one they respond to the most.

If your customers were trying to decide between a color, let's say white and dark blue, you may want to start like this:

"Let me ask you a question." What color was your last vehicle? Would you prefer a change? What color is your wife's? How about your friends or coworkers? Do you think one will create more attention when all cleaned up and out on the town?"

As your customers start to think about their answers, they will soon come up with their most preferred choice. As you begin to hear and analyze their responses, simply adjust your future questions to follow and confirm their direction. Slowly convert your discovery questions into a more leading position. Other examples may be differences such as leather versus cloth, third-row seating versus cargo space, or even a tan interior versus a charcoal interior. Know that each feature will have its own benefit and each customer will have his or her own preference.

THE PERFECT VEHICLE DOES NOT EXIST

While in the selection stage, there may also come a time when you realize your customer's perfect vehicle does not exist. It may be that all of their preferences are just not lining up. Well for this obstacle you and your customers must become aware and start to consider the closest fit. Think of it as, "Of all the vehicles you are contemplating, which would likely be your most suitable choice?" or "Of all the vehicles here, which one do you like the best?" You could actually ask this exact question.

When in this situation, let your customers know their selection might not have to be perfect. They may actually grow out of their present desires and into their next best choice. Know that many times a customer will actually leave a place of business, only to go somewhere else and purchase something completely different. You may not have the perfect vehicle, but you will often have one that they feel is close and want to consider if given the chance.

ALLOW YOUR PROCESS TO SUCCEED

Please know that not all customers are complicated in this stage. Actually, in most cases, completing this process is as simple as selecting the vehicle that has the most preferred features and separating it from the others. This step is really nothing more than a series of eliminations. If your customers are not complicated in their manner of selection, do not complicate your process. Let the selection of their new vehicle unfold by the determination of it being their most obvious choice. Okay, now for our second scenario.

2. IF YOU HAVE WHAT THEY CAME FOR, BRING THE VEHICLE TO THEM

When customers come in and ask for a specific vehicle and you have it, you want to bring the vehicle to them. You do not want to risk your customers changing their minds or confuse them by letting them wander through your inventory. If they are already decided, you do not increase their option pool, you want to keep them focused. Let them look at your photo album of customers while drinking the soda that you bought them as they await your return.

19

BE PREPARED

This is where being prepared before the customer walks in comes into play. It is essential to know your inventory. Every day before you park in the morning, slowly ride through your inventory, constantly updating your knowledge of in-stock vehicles. You should also try to attain an updated inventory list as often as you can. If a prospect wants a light-colored Explorer with gray leather, a sunroof, and rear air, you want to easily be able to check if you have one in stock. Know your available vehicles so you do not have to take the decided customer back into your inventory and risk making them undecided.

IF ONE IS VERY CLOSE, BRING IT UP

One variance for your actions with the decided customer is when you have vehicles that are close, but not exact. It is here that you would still likely be best suited to bring a vehicle up, however, you'll want to anticipate what features will least likely negate your choice. For example, your customers may be less likely to alter their preference when it comes to the style of the wheels than the pattern of the interior, or whether to include a DVD because it is already equipped with their desired sunroof, or maybe not.

Know that people can sometimes be complex when altering their preset plans. It is human nature, when making a decision, that people will often be afraid of missing something they like or paying extra for something they don't need. When determining your customer's most preferred selection, do your research in a light manner. Be careful not to push them away by forcing a decision before bringing a vehicle up. You just want to get a feel for the direction they will probably lean to best position a selection.

When you have vehicles that are very close but not exact, I have found that it is usually easier to bring one up that has an extra option or so because you can usually emotionally attach someone to an added feature if you can help them realize its benefit. I also believe that as long as they can afford it, customers will be more likely to be pleased with their future ownership if they include an option they were contemplating rather than not.

THEIR NEXT BEST CHOICE

It is essential to understand and believe that one customer's preference for a particular feature may differ from another's. The value placed on each preference and the ability to develop new desires will differ as well. Sell the inventory you have. Do not assume your customer's current or potential preferences and do not assume that they will not adjust their plans or even pay more for an additional option or benefit upon receiving new information.

Understand that you could never have every available vehicle with every possible combination of options, so be prepared to offer a new outlook when needed. Learn the features of your vehicles, know the positives they offer, and always allow the opportunity for a selection to be made.

KEEP YOUR DECIDED CUSTOMERS DECIDED

When working with decided customers, newly decided included, be sure to keep them that way. When you bring up the vehicle, make certain to keep it away from every other new vehicle parked out front. You want to limit the risk of a similar one that may draw their attention. You also in no way want to let them browse your brochures while they wait. They may want to see their selection in some new, off-the-wall color, even if they don't want that color. This could possibly give them an excuse later on if they choose to leave without making a commitment for any other reason. You want to make sure they are occupied and focused on realizing their new vehicle when you go to retrieve it. Remember, in this case, they are already decided, and you want to take every step to keep them that way.

3. IF YOU DO NOT HAVE WHAT THEY CAME FOR... OPEN THEIR OPTIONS

Treat this scenario as if your customer came in and did not know what they wanted. Get them back into your inventory. Only here, you will have to walk with a little care as you look to offer them some other options. This is not the time to say that you do not have anything for them or, "I'll see if I can find one from another dealer."

It is here that you will want to give your customers the opportunity to broaden their horizons. Take them back into your inventory and walk around to see if they land on something else. As you walk, ask the investigative questions that may uncover new or overlooked objectives.

PRESENT THE ALTERNATIVES

If someone spent some time in determining their choice, understand that they will probably be reluctant to just throw away all of their research. This customer may look to close their mind to other possibilities.

Well, it is here that you may have to realize and have your customer realize they might not be aware of all the complementary vehicles available. If they are reluctant to look at others, persuade them by explaining some possible benefits. Just say you are not completely sure of all that you have in stock and have them come with you while you check. Then slowly walk your inventory while you look for what you think might work. As you continue, look to create the questions that may change their current thoughts. Most likely, when they are surrounded by a whole new set of choices and opportunities, they'll see something else that will catch their attention. They might even find something they like better.

BE PERSUASIVE

It is human nature to be fearful of making a bad decision. Customers know this as well. So, ask yourself and ask them, what if they find and buy their envisioned vehicle somewhere else and then see one that they like better. Would they regret their decision? It is human nature that they most likely would. Remember the time you went to buy a specific television you saw in a sales catalog, but chose an entertainment center when you walked into the store? You owe your customers the same opportunity. Do not take away their ability to change their mind. Tell them this story, they will probably be able to relate to it and be more receptive to looking. When you have a settled choice, keep your customers focused. If you do not, offer them some additional choices.

Leave your dealer locate computer alone and only consider it as a last option. Too many things can happen while waiting for a vehicle to come in. Too many times, another salesperson who was willing to present them with some optional choices may influence the cancellation of your impending sale. Be committed to allowing your customers all the opportunity in the world to openly consider all of the options, features, and benefits that you and your in stock vehicles have to offer.

GAINING A COMMITMENT

Okay, now that we know the different paths of selection, it is time to understand what we must also accomplish while selecting. It is here that we must also gain a commitment to purchase if an acceptable vehicle can be found.

Many beginning salespeople will meet their customers, explain and show all of their choices, and even find a suitable solution, only to be rewarded with a thank you. To be successful, we must be better than this. We must always put our self in the best position to proceed toward actually making the sale.

Our best approach in gaining a commitment is to seek it when our customer's desire is at its highest, and this is most likely to be before their goals are met. Understand it is always easier to gain a commitment when leveraging it against a preferred, yet not realized goal, and it is also easier to move forward when you have a commitment in place upon realizing the goal.

For most people, there is a more active want factor for what is desired than for what has already been achieved. Once something is achieved, it is usually not as desirable because it already exists. You will no longer have the same ability to leverage a commitment. The curiosity in the uncertainty and the anticipation in the attainment will no longer be present with the same level of intensity.

ENACT YOUR PLAN

When seeking to gain your commitment, try to create a question that will help willingly lead them there. After discovering their needs and some initial set-up, your commitment question may go like this:

"So what you're saying is, if we were to have this model with all of your desired features, and it was available in either green, burgundy, or dark blue, you would like it, even if it were just a little over your budget. Is that correct?"

Now simply pause and wait for their answer. Then verify their commitment further by adding: "And if we were lucky enough to have it available and the terms of delivery could be worked out, you would consider owning this today, right?"

Do you see how this works? Do you see how this will both set and verify your path? Isn't it easier for them to commit before having the pressure of already finding their match?

RECOGNIZE THEIR HESITANCY

Okay, so now we know why we need to gain a commitment in the selection stage. However, for certain reasons, such as anxiety and fear, seeking our customer's commitment may be a delicate situation. Our customers may be somewhat evasive in this situation just in case they decide to leave before taking something home.

Think about it. Your customers will not want to tell you why they for some reason have decided not to buy from you down the road. They know this may produce an uncomfortable situation. They would prefer to point to a more tangible reason if this were to occur, such as not finding an agreeable choice. So, many will avoid stating their exact preferences. They were probably hassled or repeatedly asked to buy something in the past, and will seek to prevent this from happening again. Accept it, some salespeople are unskilled and unprofessional. Even most of you reading this book have had to deal with a pushy salesman before and will guard against it happening again.

It is because of this that some customers will in fact hold their goals tight or become evasive about what will work. They may even change their parameters as they go, just to stay a step ahead of actually revealing a solution. Even though your customers may know it is not the deciding moment, there will often be the hesitations that will appear. This is something we may have to contend with in every step of the process and we will have to be able to overcome it.

OVERCOME THEIR HESITANCY

However understandable our customer's motives may be, their evasiveness will often place us in a position of not reaching our goal. Because they have publicly manipulated their choices so that they will not be found, these customers will feel they would be losing their credibility by moving forward.

When in this situation, seek to understand your customers source of evasiveness. When you are able to sense the early appearance of this, you will want to investigate a little further to determine their true likes and dislikes. To best accomplish this, outwardly establish their stated likes and objections. Then take notice of any inconsistencies. Analyze each factor and search for ulterior motives. If inconsistencies come to light, question them. Then just proceed with your questions until all their responses are aligned. Once you verify and have them confirm their goals, you will then have an accurate path for your move forward.

Establishing a rapport and creating a comfortable experience will help keep your customers from becoming evasive; however, if your customers start out or become evasive, you must be prepared. This is a common obstacle and very important to understand. As far as keeping their agreement, most people will be unlikely to back out of a commitment if they have publicly agreed to it. Because again, they will want to save their credibility. If someone does back out, it will almost always be in the form of an excuse; but that's okay too, because we will investigate that as well.

Gaining a commitment is a very important concept in sales, and necessary to understand. The effect of this is considerable in helping to keep your customers moving forward in every stage. It is also one of the many factors that average salespeople never seem to fully realize. Know what is best to do and then do it. Always seek a commitment to do business if an acceptable solution can be found, and always before you complete your search.

FINAL NOTE: ALWAYS TAKE YOUR BEST PATH

The process in which you and your customers select the most suitable vehicle is basically a process of elimination. It is where you eliminate all possible choices except one and then focus on that one as their own. It's a step-by-step plan to discover, understand,

26

identify, and present the solution to their goals, wants, and needs, all while adjusting your approach. It is where every question you ask and statement you make is searching for or leading your customers toward their best choice. These three paths are your best means to select a vehicle for each situation and should be followed every time. Stay focused, remain on track, and be fully determined to find and select an agreeable vehicle.

3

PRESENT THE VEHICLE

Sales is a show. It is vital to believe that sizzle does sell. It creates the excitement that is the start for your customer's attention and desire for ownership. The vehicle is your product, and you are its spokesperson. It is now time to gain your customer's attention and create the energy and enthusiasm to attain their interest and focus.

The first thing you want to do is reset your stage. Bring the vehicle up in front of the dealership to separate it from all the other vehicles. You do not want them to lose their focus with other, similar vehicles nearby. You want them to concentrate on this one vehicle, their vehicle. Be genuinely enthusiastic about the vehicle they have selected.

ATTENTION, INTEREST, AND EXCITEMENT

Have you ever gone to a seminar and fallen asleep? Why? Was it because you weren't involved? Was it because you weren't engaged or interested?

When presenting, you are not merely presenting a vehicle, you are presenting a vehicle to a specific individual. Each person you meet will be different and each will have his or her own level of attention. Understand all of your wonderful knowledge will be wasted if your customer is not actively listening or participating.

Your first goal when presenting is to actively attain, monitor, and increase your customer's level of attention and enthusiasm. You must remain aware of how receptive your customers are and actively seek to maintain their interest. Nothing you say or show will have an impact unless they are alert and receptive.

Keep your customers involved with questions and involvement actions. Set up your presentation as a two-way conversation. Solicit feedback from your customers when demonstrating a feature and encourage them to participate. Adjust the pace and rhythm of your presentation to help create a more receptive audience. Start, stop, slow down and speed up your interaction to keep your customer's attention and keep them involved.

All customers will vary, and your presentation should be adapted just for them. Include small stories in your communication and encourage them to share their own. Understand your customers will be less likely to get bored or inattentive when sharing how they will enjoy their new vehicle than when you are just randomly listing the features of some car. Think of yourself as a talk show host, and always keep their communication flowing.

RECOGNIZE THE SIGNS

Our best source for ensuring our customer's interest is by observing and recognizing the signals they send. For example, if your customers are bored, frustrated, or confused, you will want to be able to recognize and diffuse these emotions. If they're alert, excited and interested, you will want to encourage them.

Monitor their expressions and mannerisms for the emotions they exhibit. Understand that your customer's level of participation is as important as the demonstration you are providing. In the later chapters of the book, we will learn more on how to observe and better understand our customer's emotions and take an in-depth look at recognizing and positively influencing our customer's distractions. For now though, let's continue with the presentation.

PRESENT THE BENEFITS THEY WANT

A customer's wants and needs, and their perceptions of a vehicle's benefits, are generally specific to each individual. This being the case, all professional salespeople's presentations will focus on presenting and confirming the benefits that their individual customers deem important. They will understand their customer's interests, solidify those interests, and then proceed to build upon them. If other benefits exist that you feel your customers may have interest in, seek to gauge their level of interest before deciding to what extent you will include them in your motivating efforts.

The most successful presentation is one that is catered to each customer's needs and will increase their desire to take a new vehicle home. It's also one that will entice your customer and is adapted to their personal style. Customers want a presentation that is just for them, one that is centered on the benefits they are looking for and presented in a comfortable manner. This involves demonstrating the features that will motivate their purchase while adjusting your delivery to suit their individual style.

- Recognize the benefits your customers are looking for.

- Understand how the features of your vehicle will satisfy each benefit.

- Restate the benefits your customers want, to solidify and confirm them.

- Separate each benefit and demonstrate how your vehicle will satisfy them.

- Repeat this process by continually stating, confirming, and demonstrating each benefit, thus increasing their desire and confirming their selection.

If it is important for your customer to know that their choice is proven, let them know of your vehicle's accolades. If they like the newness or uniqueness of your vehicle, sell the exclusivity of their choice. Determine the different goals your customers seek and then satisfy them. Your walk-around and demonstration should be centered on these. An effective presentation confirms how your vehicle will satisfy the wants and needs discovered while helping them select a vehicle.

Randomly listing all the features of the car is not a presentation you should consider. Understand that this presentation will sound planned and similar to any other sales pitch. These customers will feel that their salesperson does not care about their objectives or did not even listen to their requests. Often, when a sale is not made, these salespeople will not understand what they did wrong. Many will think they gave a good presentation, when actually they forgot to include the most important part; the customer.

INVOLVE YOUR CUSTOMERS AND THEIR SENSES

Physically involve your customers. Have them operate the features they are interested in. Let them open the sunroof and listen to the sound system. Ask their favorite radio stations and show them how to set them. Have them adjust the seat and the steering wheel to their liking. You want to create all the comfort and mental ownership you can.

Arouse your customer's senses. Let them smell the new car smell and experience the feeling of ownership. Understand that the senses other than hearing are often the most influential in creating an emotional interest. Include them. Do not just tell them your car has the softest leather, let them feel it. The more senses you involve, the more likely you will create the excitement needed for a sale. Create an image of where and how your customers will enjoy their new vehicle when they own it. Paint them a picture.

DRIVE THE VEHICLE

Now that we have presented and displayed our selection, it is time for them to drive their new vehicle. This is essential before you start to discuss the figures. This is where your customers will truly get to bond with their selection and can visualize ownership. Customers will want to test-drive their selection eventually, so let's do it now. This way, we will put ourselves in the position of selling a car now. Remember, now is important in our business. Continue with the flow and the idea that they are going to be purchasing a vehicle, and position yourself to do so by having them drive the vehicle. And remember, always try to go with your customers on the test drive. It is a good idea to make sure your vehicle performs as it was meant to and for you to be there for them if they have questions about operating it.

I like to have a couple of set routes for the customers to drive. Know your routes and have one for every customer. Be flexible. You might suggest a curve-filled road for a performance car or an unpaved parking lot for the four-wheel drive. For a luxury vehicle, set up a prominence route. Take them through the business district or upscale housing. Place your customers in the element they have pictured themselves in while driving their new vehicle. This will increase their visualization of ownership. If it's for hauling their kids, take them by the soccer field. If it is for recognition, have them drive through their own neighborhood. Let them wave to their neighbors from their new car. Buying a new or newer car is exciting. Let them experience the emotion and pride of their new vehicle. Give them the experience of mental ownership. Some customers may have a set plan, for them, let them drive wherever they want. If they want to show their spouse, boss, or friends, encourage it. It is good to involve other people.

If your customers are hesitant in driving their choice, be creative in your quest. If they are in a hurry, or say they are, let them know that you have a short route designed for busy people just like them. Whatever it takes, get them to drive the vehicle. Driving the vehicle is likely to be the confirmation they need to feel comfortable moving forward in the later stages. That new car smell and feel will often have a strong motivating effect.

If they are still not agreeable, offer to take them for a short ride. Then while driving, pick a nice, big, quiet parking lot, like at a mall or shopping center, and stop for one more attempt. You could always suggest a walk-around look at the vehicle and try again to switch places. While there, offer to let them drive in the parking lot. Know that most will agree to this because many times, it is just the level of traffic on the roads near the dealership that will deter them from driving. They may fear damaging your car. If their anxiety is high, seek to relax them.

GAIN THE COMMITMENT

When you are back from the test drive, pull up to the front of the store and take another walk around the vehicle. Try to gauge their level of interest in moving forward. If you feel good about it, do not hesitate in moving to the next step. Just say, "Come on in, and let's talk about it," or "Now is a good time to get your car appraised."

The conclusion of the presentation comes when your customers agree to move to the next step; when they agree to purchase the vehicle if all of the terms of delivery are agreeable. However, if they do not, the presentation stage continues. Without their acceptance of the vehicle, there is no place to go. If this is the case, you will have to continue with your presentation and gain a commitment to purchase. Be persistent in your support of their choice.

REAFFIRM THEIR SELECTION

If they are still not convinced, look to restart your presentation by rebuilding the value in their selection. Reconfirm that this is the car they selected because it has the benefits they are looking for and it completes their wants and needs. Look to influence them, using their own words. Continue to gain the small commitments necessary to move forward. Ask them the questions that will confirm their own decisions.

Your goal here is to state their desired benefits and confirm that your vehicle satisfies each of them. This is a continuous process made fresh by your use of new words and by altering your delivery. If you

34

are effective at changing your delivery, it is like offering your own second opinion; you are confirming similar information with a new conveyance. This is very effective in learning and persuasion. This, of course, must all be accomplished while still keeping their interest at a high level.

HAVE THE CUSTOMER ANSWER THEIR OWN HESITATION

One of the best ways to reaffirm your customer's selections and overcome their hesitations is with an effective series of confirming questions. This is to have your customers answer and influence themselves to overcome their hesitations with their own answers. These are more effective than your statements of satisfaction because the answer or confirmation will originate from them.

"Sir, you did say blue was the color of your choice, didn't you?" or "You stated that you liked the leather and sunroof, isn't that correct?" or "You are aware that the side-impact door beams and the side-curtain air bags provide the safety you are looking for, aren't you?"

Note that with these questions, you are getting your customers to respond positively to their selection. You are getting them to agree to the minor yeses that will lead to the bigger yes you are looking for. You are closing your customers with their own answers.

For this situation, there are many different confirmers that you can add. Wouldn't it? Doesn't it? Shouldn't it? Will it not? Don't you think? Don't you agree? Wouldn't your wife agree? There are lots of them. Rehearse some of these for your own presentations. Try to include knowledge of your customer's plans when presenting these. Simply restate their established benefits and add a confirming request.

If you don't want to overwhelm your customers with too many of these, you can switch them around. You could put them on the front or in the middle of your questions. For example, try, "Wouldn't you appreciate the peace of mind that comes with our comprehensive warranty?" or "With the fact that this model has reclining rear captain chairs and a center console, don't you think your wife will better enjoy the long trips to New England you take each fall?" If you have a good mix of these and use them in different places, your customers won't feel like they are under pressure.

Please recognize the importance of this process. I can think of nothing that has helped me sell more vehicles than what we have just gone over; the act of closing our customers with their own answers. If you think about it, there is no more effective way. Your customers will always be more persuaded by influence encouraged by you yet resolved by their own process. You are not giving your opinion or decision, you are building off theirs. You are giving them the direction and encouragement that will promote their own answers. Understand the power of this, because this is it. This is sales. This is what will give you the ability to keep your customer's forward direction at every stage of the process and will ultimately allow you to close the sale. It will not only make you a better salesperson; it will make you a salesperson. If you say it, they will question; if they say it, they will believe.

KEEP TRYING

Even if your customers have found a vehicle they truly want, their anxiety may sometimes play a role in their ability to move forward. Many customers will stall at a particular point, because they may not feel they will have the ability to slow down in the future. If this is the case, try to remove some of your customer's anxiety. Let them know that you are not looking to close the deal here, you are just trying to get to the next logical step by agreeing on a vehicle. Sometimes it helps to explain to your customers the series of steps in selling a car, and let them know that they are not owners until the final step.

When your customer is uneasy, emphasize that they're only agreeing to move forward and purchase if the figures are on their terms. They will only be buying the car if the numbers are agreeable to them. Most customers will not be afraid to move forward as long as they feel

36

they have a way out down the road. You don't always want to offer this explanation if you don't have to, but if you do you will still be in a good position because the more involved your customers become, the more likely they will follow through.

Since hesitancy in this stage is quite common and our ability to overcome their hesitancy is so important, let's pause here for a minute and try to understand our customer's frame of mind and why their anxieties may exist. The more you understand your customer's thoughts, the more you will be able to help them in moving forward. Let's take a look at an example of how one's anxiety may occur. While envisioning this example, think of your own emotions and allow yourself to try to feel what the customer might be feeling. Here we go.

Picture yourself sitting in a room. Now picture someone walking up and closing the only door. Visualize them locking the door. You are now trapped in the room with no way to get out. Has your level of anxiety increased? For most, it will.

Now let's look at the frame of mind of the person who locked the door. Do you think their anxiety level was raised?

As salespeople, we must be aware of the anxieties that the people we are working with may have, not our own. We must be able to recognize the emotions of each and react accordingly, varying our approach to each individual. If the pressure gets too high for your customers, relieve the pressure. Open the door. Do not make them stay, make them want to stay. You can always restart again. To help accomplish this, try talking to them about themselves again. Visually retake them to a comfortable place. When the pressure is relieved, try again to gain a commitment.

VARY YOUR ACTIONS

Sales is a careful balancing act. You do not want to do more than you have to, but you do want to do all that is necessary. Vary your actions. If your customers are sold, stop selling. If they are not sold, keep selling. If they are anxious, relieve the pressure. When they are at peace, start your persuasion again. Understand that if you can successfully observe, monitor, and react fittingly to the varying presence of each of your customers, you will be well on your way to increasing your sales.

Now, if they do move forward because you relieved the pressure of being committed, make sure that you continually build and then reconfirm their commitment before presenting the figures. This will help take it back to a today purchase. Once they are recommitted, be sure to confirm their recommitment.

WHAT ABOUT THE PRICE?

Note that at no point during the presentation did we discuss discounting the vehicle. If you discount the vehicle before you have a commitment or have had the proper time to build value, you will hurt your chances for a sale. You cannot sell a vehicle if the customer has not agreed upon one, and if you discount their choice before you further the value in it, any price you give will likely seem too high. If your customer brings up price, let them know that you will discuss that with them later. Always follow the steps in the process. Your first goal in selling a vehicle is to make sure they like the vehicle, and this is always to be accomplished before you discuss any discounts.

If your customer repeatedly asks about discounts, try asking them if it would be okay to discuss it later. Most of the time, these customers will appreciate the fact that you asked if it's okay, and will often be willing to discuss it later. The people who are quick to demand pricing generally feel the need to be in control, and the feeling that they decided it's okay to discuss it later is often enough control for them. Just explain that you would like some time to make sure they understand all the vehicle has to offer before you obtain a final figure.

If they insist, be strong. Let them know that you will not let price stand in the way of a deal, but you will only feel comfortable about discussing a price or discount after a specific vehicle has been chosen. Explain that you are more concerned about their lasting happiness and selecting a vehicle that is right for them, than you are about just throwing out discounted prices on unconfirmed choices. Let them know you will give them all the purchasing terms at once, without hesitation, once a vehicle is chosen.

FINAL NOTE

In sales, there are steps. Following the steps makes it easy. Giving up on the steps and losing control of the sales process will only make every step thereafter that much more difficult. Be strong and keep your steps. When presenting the selected vehicle, we want to gain our customers attention, maintain their receptiveness, present the features and benefits that are important to them, confirm their selection, and stay away from discussing discounts until we have sufficiently created a desire to own. Notice how these steps all flow together and keep the direction of the sale moving forward. Allow the steps to do the work for you. Now that you have presented their vehicle, it is time to move forward. If they have a vehicle to trade, that is where we will move next. If they do not, we will then enter the value-building stage.

4

APPRAISE THE TRADE

Think back to some of the deals that couldn't be made in your dealership's past. When asked what went wrong, how many times did a salesperson say, "Oh, we just couldn't get enough for their trade" or "They decided to keep their old car?"

Well I ask you, did the salesperson complete the proper steps in the deals they couldn't make? Did their customer really want too much, or was the salesperson just unable to sway them to a more realistic figure or depreciated sense of benefit?

INVITE THEIR DISCOVERY

In the auto business, many of our customers will have a trade, and we want to be able to properly value the trade through our customer's vision. For those of you who have been in the business for even a short time, you know all too well that nothing can ruin a deal quicker than a trade. More specifically, it is the perceived value of the trade that will cause the problem.

Okay, some appraisers are a little tighter than others, but the majority of the time it is the customer's expectations that are too high. They will often compare their vehicle to the price that others are asking for similar vehicles and expect a similar amount. However, the customer's trade is not yet a retail vehicle, and a price comparison of their vehicle should not be made with one that is ready for sale. There are a lot of expenses that go into reconditioning and inspecting a vehicle, not to mention the cost of doing business and commissions for the sale. Understand it would only make sense that the used car department is not going to pay more money for their vehicle than they would for a similar one at the auction. There is a value difference. Although your customers will probably know this to some degree, many will need some additional coaching to help accept this difference.

INFLUENCE THEIR OUTLOOK

To help accomplish our goal, we need a system in place that will help persuade our customers to accept a more realistic expectation of their trade's value. For our "persuasion stage," we will separate our effort into two steps.

First will be to complete a trade evaluation sheet with our customers where its questions are centered on searching out the trade's real condition. Next will be to walk around their vehicle, also with our customers present, taking silent notations on its signs of use. We look to involve our customers in these steps to make the revaluation more credible. In both situations, we will attempt to lower their expectations through their own perspective. Remember, if we only tell them, they will doubt it; if we involve them however, they will believe it.

THE TRADE SHEET

The first step is to ask a series of questions about their trade using a trade appraisal form as your guide. Have your customers seated and acquire their full attention. Treat this step as a very serious part of the transaction. Hopefully, the trade appraisal form that your dealer uses has more than the stats of the vehicle, but if not, you can add some of your own questions to the sheet. Make sure you have at least scanned their vehicle though, because if it is a gem, you don't want to overdo this step.

Our goal here is to ask questions that may produce realistic responses to help revise our customer's current perceived value. Here are some of the revaluing questions you can use:

Does your vehicle have a warranty?

Are you the original owner?

Does your vehicle have a salvage or flood title?

Is the odometer correct?

Has your vehicle been used in towing?

Has your vehicle ever been in an accident?

Has it ever had paint-work?

Has it ever had major mechanical repairs?

Was the problem repaired?

Is there a guarantee or warranty on that work?

Is it in need of any mechanical repairs?

Do you have the maintenance records?

When is the next maintenance due?

Very few vehicles are completely blemish-free, and almost no one keeps maintenance records. Do not comment when acknowledging their answers, just continue on as if these questions were standard procedure and very important. Picture your doctor when he asks you questions. Let out an occasional, "hmm," and keep scribbling notes. If questions arise as a result of one of their answers, question further. Put on your serious technician face.

It is very important not to draw attention to your motive. If your customers feel that this is a way of telling them their vehicle is worth less, they will argue the point. If you are effectively able to have them re-question their trade's value without you directly indicating so, you have accomplished your goal. The key is for them to come to their own conclusion so they'll be more likely to accept it as truth. You have to separate yourself and your expressions from the facts. This step is powerful. Do not skip or rush through it. Your customers will be influenced by their own answers. They will begin to realize that their vehicle is no longer new.

We are not being misleading here. Most people truly do not understand the cost of reconditioning or making a vehicle inspected and sale-ready. This is especially true if your own service department does the work. Make up some of your own questions and use them. In certain circumstances, you can adjust your line of questioning by adding, deleting, or amending your questions to fit the actual condition of the vehicle or the mindset of your customers, but do not skip this step. For example, if they are overly sensitive and start to back up on proceeding, you may choose to soften some of the questions with your manner or tone, but again do not eliminate this step. Sometimes salespeople will rush or not complete a step and still be able to make the sale, however, if you could increase your odds in making a sale every time, shouldn't you?

THE WALK AROUND

The next step is the physical involvement. This is where you and your customers will inspect their trade out in the parking lot. Ask your customers to come out with you so that you can go over their vehicle. Just say, "Come with me in case I have any questions," and start walking. It is here that you will complete your observation appraisal and hopefully confirm their perception of a lower-valued trade. This part of the show is strictly for the customer's benefit and is meant to complete the revaluation process. Start by slowly walking around the vehicle. Do not speak. Do not point out the imperfections verbally, just observe. Casually touch the paint chips. Run your hand over the crease in the body panels. Note the look of the finish. Feel the smoothness on the inside tread of the tire. Push the seat to see the severity of the wear. Look under the hood for signs of leaks or rust. Look under the car and through the wheels at the brakes. Listen to the engine. Shift the vehicle from reverse to drive. Crank the steering wheel from left to right. Listen intently while performing these steps and take notes. Look concerned and curious. Portray yourself as a technician performing an examination. Again, your goal is for them to see what you see and have them question internally what you hear. This part of the step is so important. Understand that your customers may actually be seeing the signs of wear for the first time.

Although the overall condition may be readily apparent to them with the completion of this process, you should always make a special effort to establish the vehicle's mechanical shape. This is often what is most important when appraising its real value and is many times unknown or overlooked by your customers. Remember to be focused while you listen to the engine. Many motors will have some funny noise if you listen close enough, and many will also have some type of clunk when going in and out of gear. If and when they hear something, they won't bring it up either, but they will likely make a mental note of what they hear. When you have hundreds of parts, you're going to have the potential for some foreign noises. If a problem is detected, let them hear it now. The effect this will have on the perceived value of their trade will be more persuasive and better timed than if brought up later while presenting the figures.

Most people are so involved with everyday life that they will not notice all of the wear and tear their vehicle has, or they may just simply get used to it. With a proper walk around, however, they will be forced to realize it. Not only will you help revalue their trade here, in many cases, you will further present the case for them to purchase sooner than later. Although you should never ask what a person wants for his or her trade, because it allows them to set the standard, sometimes people will force it on you. When this happens, watch how many people will lower their stated value before you even finish this step and without you even saying a word. All top salespeople know the power of this step and will take the control needed to complete it. Do not let your customers or lack of process convince you to skip this or other indispensable steps by indicating or thinking that nothing matters but the final figures. In fact, this is exactly how your best chance of coming together is achieved. Always prepare yourself to make a sale. Do not eliminate or degrade the steps that will assist you in preparing for a more compliant audience.

FINAL NOTE

When negotiating the terms of your transaction, the price of your vehicle and the price for their trade will mean nothing unless they are in some way attached to a perceived value. It is your job as the salesperson to help attach the proper value in each. With these steps, you are successfully placing a value on their trade and in cases where their trade warrants a revaluation, as it often does, you are more than likely lowering their expectations. Completing this step can be the difference in making a profit or even making a deal. Do not diminish the need for this step, and remember above all else, this is a silent valuation. You want to effectively lower their perception without telegraphing your intention or putting your customers in a defensive position.

Learn to make your deal here. Your newly created valuation difference is most likely to be the difference that exists later on in your negotiation. Always take the necessary control and complete the steps that will aid you in reaching a deal. Always evaluate their trade where they are included. Now you can drive the car over for the official appraisal.

5

BUILD VALUE

Value is everything in our business of sales. It is what our customers must feel a sense of before they will ever consider initiating a purchase. Without value, there can be no basis on which to state a fair price for any product. The purpose of this chapter is to help prepare for the negotiation stage by building value in yourself and in your dealership, the added value needed to make a sale.

In any form of sales, value is recognized as the measure of a product's worth. This value may be recognized by discernible factors such as performance, efficiency, and safety, or emotional factors such as enjoyment, status, and peace of mind. Note that these factors are common to all types of sales because they're directly related to the product being offered. Meaning, a typical product could literally sell or not sell by being what it is. Think of when you go to a grocery store or toy store. In vehicle sales however, the sales experience itself will often account for much of a person's decision-making process as well. It is here that the value of purchasing and owning a particular vehicle is either enhanced or diminished.

The value created in a vehicle sales experience is often measured by additional variables that a consumer will take into account before making a purchase. These variables are you, and your dealership. It is because of these two variables, there will always be different levels of performance within your sales department. The salesperson with the superior ability in adding value to their sales equation will consistently sell the most vehicles and be the most profitable.

There are many competing dealerships with similar vehicles and similar prices. To perform at a high level, you have to set yourself and your dealer apart. True vehicle sales ability, although a combination of many individual factors, is ultimately the ability to provide a perception of additional value. Although many of the product-specific constants of our vehicles are similar to other products, it is often the established value of you and your dealership that are the most influential in when, where, and why people buy their new vehicle. The more value you build in the service that you and your dealership provide, the more likely your customers will buy.

All average salespeople believe that their customer's perceptions of value lie only in what is being offered and for how much. They will often choose to skip this step and instead take the customer's preferred route of just discussing price. All top salespeople however, have come to realize the importance of this step and will place the emphasis on value in themselves and in their dealerships. They understand this additional value's powerful influence and will take the time and effort needed to create it. An excellent time to build the value of yourself and your store is after the presentation and before you start to prepare the figures. Let's take a look.

SELL YOURSELF

Present yourself as someone who wants to and is able to help them through the proper evaluation of their needs with the credible advice that you offer. A professional who understands your customers and the vehicles you represent. Give them the confidence to accept your advice. Let your customers know that you will be there for them before and after the sale. Take the time to establish common ground and build rapport. Develop an understanding of their needs and have empathy for their concerns.

Your customers are not just buying a car, they are buying you; a salesperson they can trust and count on. Let them know how long you have been at your dealership and the commitment you have to be there. Let them know you're there for your current customers and you will be there for them. Provide the awareness that if they buy another vehicle from another dealer, they will not have you or your service.

The salespeople who genuinely care for the people they meet are often the most successful. This is because this trait will come out in their presence. For these salespeople, because they enjoy meeting people, they will naturally increase the value in their experience. This in turn, will often make price less important in their customer's eyes and less likely to be an objection in the later stages. Take the lead from these salespeople. Attach an importance to your customer's experiences, not just the sale price. Have your customers realize the benefit of having you as a salesperson and seek to integrate it into their decision-making process. Let them think of you as a plus to the sale, not indifferent or worse, a minus. If you are effective at this, please know that many will buy from you and only you, in fact, actually making you part of the sale.

EVIDENCE MANUAL

Creating the evidence that you've helped people in the past goes a long way with your current customer's perceptions of how well you will help them in the future. One such way is to build your own evidence manual. This can be achieved in no better way than with a photo album of your previous customers. Know that it's never too early or late to start a photo album of your happy, smiling customers. When looking through your album, your potential future customers will picture themselves in the photos you share, and this will help your credibility. Start with a small album and move to a larger one as you get more pictures. Start today.

When your customers see people just like themselves purchasing the vehicles you sell, they'll feel more comfortable with the quality of service you provide and the acceptability of the vehicles you offer. They will also feel more compelled to do business with you, because people like doing business with successful people. Your photos will show that you successfully make people happy. They will want to share the feeling your customers show in your pictures. Remember, everybody smiles for the camera.

SELL THE DEALERSHIP

An excellent time to build further value in your dealership is while you are having your customer's trade appraised or after you've demonstrated the selected vehicle. Remember, this step should always be taken before you attempt to negotiate the figures. If you do not take the time to add value to their purchase before you present your figures, the offered price will always seem too high. Just let your customers know that their trade's appraisal can take between ten and fifteen minutes, and take this time to build the value needed to ensure a sale.

Here is where you will want to establish the bond between your customers and your dealership's family home. A good start for this would be to walk your customers to the concession area and buy them a drink and maybe a snack. Have your customer feel at home. Use your own money for their refreshments. Show your customers that you are willing to invest in your relationship. This will help most people better connect with you, as they will appreciate your efforts. Besides, it is the mentality of most to return the favor in some way. Have you ever received an unexpected Christmas card and hurried out to get one for the sender? You probably have. It's a natural reaction. Often, people will look to give something back. And of course the gift we want is their time and attention.

From the concession area, proceed to the service department and give them a tour. Let them know where they'll be getting their car serviced. Show them all the state-of-the-art service equipment and modern tools that your dealership has to offer. Let them know that your dealership is capable of properly handling the service needs of their new vehicle, and that they will be well taken care of should something go wrong. Show them the customer waiting area and the free coffee machine. Let them see all the service awards and certifications of the mechanics employed at your dealership. Let them know how seriously your service department takes customer satisfaction. Show them all of the nice letters your service department has received over the years.

Introduce them to the service cashier and the service manager. They will always be nice and courteous to their potential new customers. In addition, since they won't have the anxiety of the sale, their interaction will generally be relaxed. They will almost invariably ask, "What model have you purchased?" This is great because it will always come out sincere. This is one more step in building mental ownership for your customers.

This is also people involvement. The more people you involve, the more involvement your customers will have. This has the same effect as the neighbor close, where you let your customers take their pending solution home for a solo demonstration and their friends or neighbors will see them. Now that they have met your service staff, they too will be involved in your customer's ownership of that vehicle. Additionally, since your fellow coworkers will always have something nice to say about the chosen vehicle, this will be like getting a second opinion or a reaffirmation of their decision.

SELL THE WHOLE EXPERIENCE

What you are doing here is setting the stage. You are building value. If you do a good job at this, the negotiation stage will become the easy stage. People will appreciate and pay for good service. Learn to realize and portray that the most important option your customers will be getting in their transaction is the benefit of having you and your dealership. Let them know that you will be there for them, let them know that your service manager will be there for them, let them know your whole team will be there for them. Tell them how long your dealership has been a part of the community and how they support the local teams, groups and charities. Be enthusiastic in your efforts. Understand that price is not the determining factor in someone purchasing from you or your competitor; it is the quality of their experience and the value of the service that you and your dealership represent. Walk them through the night-drop. Introduce them to the receptionist, the parts department, and their new service writer. Show them that you and your dealership are one big happy family, and then make them feel that they are a part of your family as well.

Have you ever paid more for something because of the quality of service you received? Of course you have. So will they. In car sales, this is the value that counts.

6

PREPARE FOR THE NEGOTIATION

When you and your customers have settled on a specific choice, it is time to invite them in to work out the details of delivery. It is time for you to present the figures. However, before you will ever be able to sell a car, you will first need an able participant to sell to. It is here that you must determine that your customers are both able and willing to purchase before you start to write the deal or negotiate the terms.

Please understand that this is a critical time in our process. It is absolutely essential that you verify their commitment to purchase before you give them any discounted or final pricing information. You have to analyze the intentions of your customers before proceeding. Because, make no mistake, if you offer the final figures without a commitment or an ability to purchase, you will end up with what you started with; nothing. They will thank you for your information and leave.

PREPARE YOUR PLAN

It is at this stage that our customers will usually have one of three plans. They will either want to walk in and sign the papers, want to negotiate the purchase to buy, or want to negotiate with no intention of making a purchase. Our goal in preparing for this stage is to determine which of these is our customer's plan. We want to know how to proceed before we do proceed, because it is with each of these scenarios that we will want to approach uniquely.

ASSUME THE SALE

First of all, if they are willing to purchase without objection, we do not want to inhibit them by presenting an option to negotiate. Give your customers the opportunity to walk in and purchase. If they are agreeable to just filling out the necessary papers, we want to let them. The best way to accomplish this is to assume that they will.

Note that it is here that many inexperienced salespeople will incur an obstacle just by presenting negotiation as an option. Do not do this. If they are willing to just write it up, write it up. Always imply that you are only proceeding to complete the necessary paperwork. Make this your process, rather than asking for their acceptance of the price. Let them bring up negotiating a price as a condition of the sale.

ARE YOU READY TO NEGOTIATE?

Although we should always assume the sale, we will often be in a position where our customers will want to negotiate the figures. If this is the case, stop and make sure you are ready to proceed. Analyze your customer's intentions. You want to know if you have a commitment and the ability to make a sale exists, before you start to work out the details. Otherwise, you will have lost all of your leverage to influence one.

It is also at this stage that you'll want to know all the parameters needed to make a sale. Always seek to tie up all the loose ends to avoid any unforeseen future objections or openings that will give them the excuse not to move forward later on. Remember, many people do not come in to negotiate to buy. They come in to see what you have, get your best figures, and then go to the next dealer to see if a better deal is available. It is often their intention to shop around before they commit. However, it is our goal to get them to buy now, while they are here. So, let's prepare.

PREPARE TO SUCCEED

The best way to succeed is to know and meet the conditions of the sale up front and verify a commitment to do business today if the

54

numbers work out. In addition to having completed all of the preceding steps of the sale, you must also be able to answer these questions before a negotiation can take place.

1. Is there a trade involved?
2. Are all the decision makers here?
3. Are they ready to do business now?

KNOW IF THERE IS A TRADE

Your customer's trade is a condition or parameter of the sale. Although it's not an objection of doing business, it is still necessary to know up front. You always want to include all price-related variables in the presented figures. If you do not, you will have to renegotiate for every variable added.

In some cases, you may have to investigate. Ask them what they are driving now and what they plan to do with it. Analyze their answer for the truth. Make sure it makes sense. Know that some customers will hide their trade until the last minute so they can negotiate twice. This is often suggested by the car buying books so they can have a more accurate means to comparison shop. However, it is our goal to make a deal now.

HAVE ALL THE DECISION MAKERS PRESENT

Before you continue, you have to determine if all the decision makers are present. This is where our first rule of negotiation applies.

No ability to make a decision equals no sale. There is no reason to proceed and negotiate if a decision cannot be made.

To accurately determine this, you will probably have to investigate here as well. Start by asking if anyone else will be involved in the purchase. If their answers are hesitant or non-specific, expand your inquiry. If your customer outwardly states that no one else is involved, they will be less likely to use this as an excuse to leave after you present them with the figures. If your customer states that there are other decision makers, try to determine if there really are, or if this is just a stall. Question this and seek out the truth as well. Know that different customers will often have different motives and plans when it comes to their negotiating goals and each goal must be determined before you can proceed.

If there is another party that has to be involved, make every attempt to have the other party present before you present the figures.

Know that having a decision maker not there will always be the opening they need to leave once they have your figures, and this is what we are trying to avoid.

Offer to let your customers take their selected vehicle to pick the other party up. Offer to go with them. Offer to let your customers use your phone and call the other party to come down. If they cannot, ask if they can get the okay to make their own decision while on the phone. This other party may be the customer's spouse, neighbor, boss, son, or financial advisor. Be persistent in getting the other party there. Do not let your customers take the figures to the other party. It's unlikely that they will be able to present all of the information gathered as well as you. Let your customers know that if another person really is a decision maker, he or she should see the vehicle too, and have the opportunity to have any of his or her questions answered before being asked to make a decision.

If all else fails, schedule a new time when all the parties can be present, and leave some information out or the terms open to insure your customer's curiosity. Know they will be less likely to come back if the feel that they already have all the answers they need. Take every step possible to ensure their return. Understand if you give figures to people who are unable to come to terms, you will have greatly limited their chances of coming back. When they do meet up with their other party, they will probably check with another dealer to see if they can get a better deal. Trust this. And oh, guess what? They almost surely can. Some dealer somewhere will always be able to beat your deal. Do not lose your deal here. Persuade your customers to have all of their participating decision makers present before you agree to negotiate.

COMMITMENT BEFORE FIGURES, NO EXCEPTIONS

Once we have established if there is a trade, and if all of the decision makers are present, it will be our goal to do business now. We will want to make a deal if the figures are acceptable. However, in order to accomplish this, we as well will also need to have a willingness to do business.

Even if we have expertly performed all the previous steps, there still may be the customer who is not ready to commit to a purchase. If this is the case, we must do all we can to influence them into allowing themselves to make a decision. This is where our second rule of negotiation applies. No commitment also equals no sale. If you give out figures without first obtaining a commitment to buy, you'll have given up all chances of holding any gross, and in many cases, will have lost the deal. You will have completed all of the work in selecting and presenting and yet will basically be handing the deal to your nearest competitor. Understand that this is what the skilled shopper wants. They want to come in, get all the information they can, and then leave for the next dealer to see if they can get a better price. These are the customers you need to be able to sell. This is when you must not lose trust in your process or allow yourself to be persuaded. Price out of place will decrease your chances of making a sale. We are not in the business of giving out shopping figures; we are in the business of finding the best vehicle for our customers and having them purchase from us. Always take the path to success, not the path of least resistance. Please understand that it is pointless to negotiate on price when you don't have a commitment to purchase or if the ability to reach a decision doesn't exist.

Having the knowledge and resolve to trust and follow this process is the difference between the top performer and the average order taker. Think this out and understand it. Be strong and follow the rules for your best chance of making a sale. Follow the process. Many of your customers will say they just want the figures so they can think, however, the odds are great that they'll compare your numbers and make a decision without giving you a second chance. Prepare yourself beforehand, because you will soon be in this position.

INFLUENCE THE COMMITMENT

The best time to make a deal is now. To help further persuade your customers for a now decision, start with the reaffirmation of their choice as discussed in the presentation chapter. Confirm that it satisfies their wants and needs and that it's their selected vehicle. Since they have successfully selected a vehicle, explain that this is the next logical step.

If you feel your customers are really ready and just need a little pushing, repeat that they'll only be purchasing if the figures are on their terms. Persuade them into a commitment by emphasizing that they still control the decision. This is another example of relieving the pressure enough for them to move forward. If you don't think your customers are ready, revert to the presentation or value stage until they are. Continue building your rapport to establish the working relationship you will need to continue. The more comfortable they feel working with you, the more time and credence they will give you.

If a commitment still cannot be reached, with your manager's permission, let them take their selected vehicle home overnight and set an appointment for the next day. If you know they're able to buy and really in the market, having them take the vehicle home is the best way to keep them involved. If needed, let them know that there are a couple of good reasons for them to take the vehicle. One is that everyone should feel comfortable with what they are purchasing. Also, if another party does need to be involved, this is a great opportunity to show the vehicle in a neutral setting. There is no better close for customers that are almost there. The odds are in your favor that they will bond with their selection. The longer your customers are involved with their choice, the more comfortable they will become with it.

58

For the undecided customer, this is often a helpful extension of your presentation or test drive. It also creates the opportunity for the involvement close. When your customer is at home and they look out and see their choice in their driveway, it may become their own. It may be that they are already involved with their new vehicle. If this is the case, they won't let you take their vehicle back. Also, when their neighbors see them in their new vehicle, your customers will likely realize that they like being seen in it. People like the status of having a new vehicle and will not want to give that status up. I think it is safe to say that many people you'll meet are at least somewhat image or attention conscious. In any case, if they take the vehicle off your lot, the odds of them coming back are obviously good, and this is what you want. If you are unable to gain a now commitment, or if the customer is limited in their ability to purchase, your best chance will be to create a second chance.

An additional benefit for your customers reasoning would be if they were to have a trade. Point out that by taking your vehicle home and leaving their trade, you will be able to show it to your buyers and possibly get more money for it. Explain to your customers that the more money you can get for their current vehicle, the more money you can give them when presenting your figures. Be persuasive. Let them know you'll work hard to obtain a higher offer when presenting it. Let them know that from past experience, you are usually able to receive more when your auto brokers can see and drive the trade in person. Also, because they are leaving undecided, this will create a variable in the equation that will help keep their curiosity. If a trade exists, give your customers the benefit of a better deal.

STILL NO COMMITMENT

In certain cases, some customers may be very challenging. They may agree that they like and want the vehicle they have selected, but will still want the figures without giving a commitment. These are typically your price buyers and skilled shoppers.

Understand that with this customer, price curiosity is the only leverage you have. Do not give in. Do not lose your deal here. Work to get a commitment first. Do not let your emotions get the better of your actions, simply state that you will not negotiate on a vehicle until they have considered ownership. Explain that you and your owner feel that it is important for future customer satisfaction that their customers are sure they will be happy with the vehicle and willing to own before you discuss a discounted figure. Explain that some customers get caught up in the negotiation, buy the vehicle, and then regret their choice later. Explain that this will ultimately result in a dissatisfied customer, and that is something that you and your dealership want to avoid.

Make no mistake, you will also get the customer who will demand a sale price, even though they will not give a commitment. Some customers feel it is their right. It is not. Search out their true intentions. Do not give out discounted shopping figures; no ballpark figures either. Understand a ball park figure is often enough for some to justify a comparison and purchase elsewhere. Others will try to convince you that they won't go anywhere else to leverage your numbers. They just want to analyze their budget. Don't readily believe them. This is untrue about 95% of the time. Follow the odds. Offer to help figure out their budget with them. Be strong. Do not let them convince you otherwise. Always obtain an agreement to do business before you present the figures.

TRUST THE PROCESS

You have to be strong and trust the process. I know this might be hard for the new salesperson to understand, but it is essential if you are to be successful. Most beginning salespeople are fresh and full of enthusiasm. Unfortunately, they also typically believe that the best way to sell a car is to do everything the customer asks, and this is not always true. Understand that some customers are skilled shoppers who are very good at hiding their true intentions. Only the most skilled salesperson knows that the easiest way to sell a car is to do what is right to sell a car, not necessarily what the customer says will sell the car.

What may make this even harder for new salespeople to grasp is if they actually do make a sale without following the process. However, what they must understand is, there will always be some who will come in and buy, no matter what you do. So just because you sold a car without following the process does not mean the process is not your surest route to additional sales. Trust the process and stick to it. Stay with the odds. I know of no one who is so fortunate that they can consistently perform without following the process. If you were successful in accurately determining your customer's needs and able to help select the vehicle they would like to own, you deserve the sale, not your competitor. Work to encourage your customer's commitment.

UNDERSTANDING YOUR CUSTOMER'S THOUGHTS

There is a reason that some of our customers will want a price and then want to leave. They won't want to buy a vehicle and learn later that they could have gotten a better deal elsewhere. They want to be able to tell their friends that they got a good deal, and shopping around is the best way to accomplish this. However, most customers really don't want to take the time and effort to shop around, they just want to avoid the thought of not getting a good deal. So, know your efforts to persuade will often be well received. If you have followed all of the steps of the sales process up to this point, don't be shy, ask for the agreement you need to complete the sale.

There are generally two approaches that shopping customers will present when they want to leave and compare figures. In the first, these customers won't want to offend and will say that they want to think about, or sleep on the figures. In the second, they will tell you straight out that they'll be shopping your figures. In either case, however, if they leave with a discounted figure, they will probably not be back.

They'll either have what they want or will soon realize they have something they can use and will head to the next dealer. Please know that it's these objections that you will have to be able to overcome before you can make a sale. Fortunately, these are some of the objections that we will be learning how to overcome in more detail in the upcoming chapters. Have patience, we're almost there.

FINAL NOTE

The art of selling cars is a progression of actions and reactions, all while staying within the main parameters of the plan. Notice that this stage of the sales process involves a series of steps to put yourself in the best situation by not giving up everything at once. There is a definitive response for every action our customers take. The closer we follow the path to the sale, the better chance we have to selling them a car. Be strong, be confident, and remain in control. Always take the steps to succeed. Get a commitment to purchase and verify the ability to purchase before you present the figures. Understand it is us who must provide the atmosphere and the process that will influence our customers and allow them to change their parameters as they go.

Now that we have completed this step of the process, we are ready to present the figures. However, before you do, stop here once again to be absolutely sure that you are best prepared to continue by having completed all of the preceding steps of the process. At this point, the steps, in order, are: greet and build rapport, select a vehicle, present and drive the vehicle, create value, "value" the trade, and of course, prepare to negotiate. Okay, let's present some figures.

7

PRESENT THE FIGURES

Presenting the figures should be one of the easiest steps in the sales process. However, this is often the step that will provide the most anxiety for the beginning salesperson. This is because they will not set themselves up to succeed. Top salespeople however know that they must prepare to succeed. They will have a set plan and will follow it every time.

There are three key rules to follow to best prepare yourself to present the figures.

They are:

- Follow the steps of the sale to build value first.
- Stay away from discussing discounts before presenting the figures.
- Always use a worksheet to present the figures.

If you start the steps with the negotiation in mind, you'll be better able to understand the direction of your path and stay on track. When you're set to present the figures, they should always be presented with a form or worksheet. The same worksheet should be used every time, so you can become comfortable and fluid in using it.

The place to start is with the full list price, or full retail value. If you know that every time you open a deal, it will be at the list price, you'll be less likely to cut corners in the process. This will help condition yourself to stay away from discussing discounts out in the parking lot. Keep them curious, and you will keep their attention. Give them all the information up front and their curiosity will lead them to visit the next dealer. Additionally, if you do discuss discounts, you will no longer be able to use your worksheet effectively. You'll have already adjusted your figures and have eliminated its use. This is where you will lack the fluidness and control that you would have had with the worksheet.

I have visited many dealerships and found that most worksheets are very similar. Most dealerships will have some common form or script to present the figures. They will usually include the vehicle and customer information, followed by a word-track that helps deliver the figures in a structured fashion. However, I have also found that in most stores, these worksheets never leave the shelves they rest on. They are never used. Well, this is crazy. Set yourself apart and take the best path to increase your profit and the likelihood of a sale. Always use a worksheet to present the figures. If your dealership is strict about following the worksheet, good for them. If they are not, or don't have one, make one up for yourself using the information listed here as a guide.

OUR GOAL IS ONE STEP AT A TIME

Our main objective when presenting the figures should be to transition our customers into the business office. In fact, this should be our only goal. We simply want to get an agreement on the sale and trade figures in order to proceed to the next step. Let your business manager handle the correlating interest rates, warranty prices, and payments. Yes, most customers will make their buying or budget decisions based on a payment, so we want to close to a payment; however, the business office should handle that part of the transaction. We do not want to wrap up all the financial terms of the delivery at our desks. We just want to continue the process. You can even explain this to the customer. The business manager has the relationships with the banks, knows the interest rates, and has the information needed to offer other available products, such as extended warranties or other coverage. For the most part, this won't limit management's ability to make any final adjustments necessary to conclude a transaction and will keep you from trying to determine how much of a payment your customer is willing to accept.

Another reason for keeping these final terms relegated to separate steps is to provide a fresh face, one that is not tainted and has not witnessed what the customer demanded or stated earlier about their financial goals. This allows the finance manager to have no preconceived notions and will also allow your customer to change their parameters without losing their credibility. Simply put, your customers may agree to a higher payment or alternative terms with less hesitancy because they won't have to back down from what they earlier told you. Because of course, you are no longer present or involved. In addition, the business managers are usually some of the best closers in the business and can take over with a new aura of control. They will be rested, in the comfort of their offices, and more attuned to completing this final step.

In some cases, certain customers will push for the payment, the interest rate, or an approximate price on an extended warranty up front. Do not give in. Keep to your steps of the sale. We are best advised to keep their curiosity active throughout each step so that we can more easily lead them to the next step. Also, be forthright about the fact that your dealership takes very seriously the confidentiality of their financial information; therefore, it is discussed only by qualified professionals and in the business office. Let them know that there are no exceptions.

OFFER UP THE FIGURES

When presenting the figures, we want to list all of the figures at once in a set format. We want to list the full retail price, any manufacturer rebate, the value of the trade, the amount of the down payment, and the monthly terms that the business office will use to calculate our customer's payments. I assume your worksheet has the basic vehicle and prospect information, so I will start from there.

List in order:

- The full list price of the vehicle you're selling.
- The manufacturer rebate. Dealership discount if a pre-owned vehicle.
- The resulting sale price.
- The value of the customer's trade.
- Payoff difference, to be deducted from the sale price.
- The amount of down payment requested.
- The monthly terms your business office will use for payments. For example, forty-eight, fifty-four, and sixty months.

Once you add some blanks and include the connecting phrases that you're comfortable with, your presentation sheet is finished. You now have a permanent word track that will smooth your customer's transition into the business office. Remember; always portray this as just a step to get to the next step. Get your customer to agree to do business at the figures your manager has filled in for you. Keep your job limited to the figures. Even if they are cash buyers, you should still use this sheet. Let the business office handle how they will arrange payment.

FOLLOW THE SCRIPT

A good idea for newer salespeople, or for those who are not confident at this stage, would actually be to read the finished script, word for word, right to the customer. When doing so, read it as though you have to read it, as though reading it is one of the dealership's mandatory steps. What this will do is give you strength. It will keep you uniform and stable. It will take away much of your fear and not let your thoughts or lack of assurance show in your delivery. Know that this is where fear strikes many beginning salespeople. Reading it word for word however, will often let the fear out. This will also take you out of the equation in the event that they are upset with the figures presented. You didn't write these figures, you are just completing a step. This will allow you to still be the good guy and keep your position as someone who wants to help them come to an agreement.

ASK FOR THE SALE

After you have read the manager's figures, pause briefly and then calmly ask for their agreement. It might go like this, "All right, all I need is your okay, and we can finish up the paperwork for the business office." Then, with very little pause and while you are casually straightening your paperwork, continue with, "Let me have a copy of your driver's license to get started, and if you could, let me get you to put down a little info on this." Hand them a credit statement or insurance form and start filling out the order. If there is no objection, don't give them one. Assume there is none and continue moving forward.

When completing your presentation of the figures and asking for the sale, it is very important to show an even temperament. Do not act any differently. Act as this is a natural occurrence and that everybody agrees to the presented figures. Customers are sharp and will sense any unevenness in your actions, so focus on staying composed. Also, try to know your forms well so you can continue with small talk while completing them. You always want to get as much of the deal written as quickly as possible, while the customer is still occupied, so make sure to give them another form if they finish early. Once they consent to an agreement or state no more objections, continue at a calm, but rapid pace. Do not give them the opportunity to go backwards. Get the paperwork complete, have the manager sign it, and take the folder to finance.

RECOGNIZE AND ENCOURAGE THEIR WILLINGNESS

When presenting the figures, if your customers are willing to move forward, move forward. Let them consider the payment and relating terms as the condition of doing business. Note that not all customers are difficult in proceeding. In fact, you should assume that they are not. Go over all figures with complete confidence. The goal of this book is for you to learn to sell the tough deals, however, always assume that the customer will do business at the figures offered and complete the transaction in the business office.

Sometimes, for unsure customers, it may help to portray our presentation of the figures only as a step that is necessary to complete before we can go to the next step. As discussed earlier in agreeing on a vehicle and gaining a commitment, they are not committed to purchase, even if they agree to the figures here. Explain again that you are just trying to get them to this next logical step; the business office. It is here, too, that you'll want to vary your actions according to your present situation.

KEEP YOUR CLOSED CUSTOMERS ACTIVE

If your customers do not readily close here, that's okay. The chapters in closing and overcoming objections are soon to come. If the customer does close however, you want to continue to keep them active right up until they sign the official paperwork. This is very important and worth repeating. Get your customers a box to gather up items from their trade or have them transfer insurance information from your phone. Always be sure that their attention is diverted from the decision they have just made. If they are left alone or inactive, their anxieties may start to kick in. They may lose their devotion to both you and the deal. If you involve them, however, they will feel more comfortable and less likely to rethink their decision. Also, by keeping them involved and committed, they'll be more likely to accept the terms when in finance.

Place your photo album in front of them and see if they recognize anyone. Let them look at your happy, smiling customers one more time as reassurance for their impending experience. If the wait for finance is a little long, reintroduce them to the service department or other parts of the dealership. The more comfortable they feel in their surroundings and the more support they have, the more flexible they'll be if payment is an issue. When the business office is ready, walk them in, and introduce them. Make sure the vehicle is being prepared as you get the owner's manual and spare keys ready. Then just listen for the sweet music of the printer.

WORKSHEET WITH A PURPOSE

The goal of our worksheet is to offer a structured plan to present the figures in an easy fashion. It's also to create the position of influence for some of our most effective closes if needed. Of course, our first goal is to have our customers close on the terms presented; however, we also want to create the best situation in case they do not. We have to position ourselves if they want to negotiate.

Our first objective in creating our future opportunities is to help construct the often-needed curiosity by leaving the final terms undetermined. As stated earlier, our main goal here is to have our customers proceed into the business office, and creating this curiosity will help drive their willingness.

Our second objective is to draw their attention to one specific variable as our closing point of contention. This will help narrow their focus, thus subconsciously allowing their acceptance of the other variables. This makes sense, right? Only seek to tie one loose end at a time and always seek to eliminate the questioning of additional variables as you do.

If they are financing and not readily closing, try to steer their focus to the payment. Use this to get them into the business office. Gain their acceptance to write the deal up as it is and submit it to finance. Let their curiosity lead them there. For these customers, just say, "Okay, let me get some necessary information for our business office, and they can get started determining the payment terms that will best work for you."

If the customer's primary concern is not payment, single out the remaining factor they seem concerned with the most. This is usually the amount of their down payment, their trade value, or your listed price, and is simply accomplished by over or undervaluing the selected variable. One example would be to set the trade value overly low or the down payment overly high. Know it is always easier to negotiate and reach an agreement when you have narrowed the number of variables down to one. If you can predetermine their most likely concern before you present your figures, you can better set yourself up by leaving the most room to play within that specific variable. If their main focus is limited in room to play, such as an advertised sale price, or if they have a written trade appraisal from another dealer, then listing a substantial down payment will usually get their attention. In addition to narrowing the field, adjusting the down payment saves adjusting your figures for last, and only if necessary.

If they're unresponsive to the down payment, try to verify their next biggest point of concern and focus on that as the only condition of the sale. Always imply consent with the other variables involved. From here, you can now focus on closing the deal by negotiating the one remaining variable. This, of course, will be the focus of the upcoming chapters.

WHERE IS THE CASH FROM?

Before moving on to any of the other variables make sure you have sufficiently allowed your customers to let the payment be the deciding factor. Also, be sure that if they are cash buyers, you research how they're obtaining their cash. Determine if it's from their savings or if they have arranged outside financing. If they've arranged outside financing, allow them the opportunity to have your business office arrange a financing plan for them. Explain that you may be able to offer them comparable or even better terms and that this way, all the paperwork can be handled accurately and completed right away. Additionally, you can promote the benefit of them keeping their source of financing for future wants or needs by using one of your sources. This may actually convert them to finance buyers and precipitate a less resistant path to the business office. It will also be easier to offer an extended warranty and other available items that they might like to have by creating and adjusting the final terms with their preferred budget in mind.

THE KEY TO THE FIGURES

The whole setup of this chapter and your ability to double your present sales is based upon one thing; having the ability to stay away from price before it's time. It is not discussing a discounted price before you have established your customer's desires, created a sense of value within them, and last but not least, determined that an ability to purchase is present. This element is so important in the sales process, yet it's still the one most salespeople are never able to accept or successfully follow. Because this is so significant, I feel it is worth a further look. This time, let's seek understanding from a salesperson's point of view. I will try to explain in more detail the reason I believe we find this so difficult to accept, and why we should. Here we go.

Some salespeople will rationalize not following the steps and discuss discounts before they should because they will want to please their customers. They will skip the steps or allow a price discussion because they let their customers take control of the pace and structure of the sale. They want to satisfy their consumers by answering all of their questions and providing all of the information requested. However, these salespeople are unable to separate the early stage of the process, where it is imperative to listen to and understand their customer's needs from the later stage, the buying stage. I understand that this may be difficult, but if you want to be successful, you have to be strong and do what is best to help you sell more cars. You have to separate the stages. There is a time to listen and a time to take control.

Once you have listened to your customer's needs and selected the best possible vehicle for them, it is time to lead, not follow. Stay away from discussing a discount until it's time. I understand that there may be a temptation for less-skilled salespeople to skip this advice, but in almost all cases, understand that most customers will usually only present a limited challenge here. Have the ability to recognize this and remain consistent in your efforts to move past their influence and hold on to your price. Assess the customer's needs, select a vehicle, and build value. Allow them and yourself the opportunity to justify the list price before you start to dismiss it. Most customers will readily follow your process if it is presented properly. Only customers who have little or no intention of buying from you anyway will continue to press you for your lowest price up front, right now, immediately. And it is with these markedly insistent customers that you must be the most aware, because with them, price is your only leverage.

Another reason some salespeople will offer early discounts is because they want to appear knowledgeable of the pricing possibilities or show that they have the power to discount. Their self-image is more important than their desire to make a sale. These salespeople might not even be aware that this is costing them deals. However, they will not excel in sales until they are able to alter their thinking. All top salespeople are aware of this and have decided that helping find a proper solution and taking the best path to make a sale is what really matters. They know that being smart is more effective in sales than trying to appear smart. Your goal as a salesperson should be to help your customers find the most suitable vehicle and then have them purchase from you. Your goal should not be to do all the work in selecting a vehicle and then direct your customers to purchase somewhere else by giving them a price to shop around with, or by lessening their desire or interest in purchasing by eliminating their curiosity

Always leave open the ability to start the negotiation at the full list price. Do not give in to the requests that will hurt your chances.

Give yourself the time to build value, ensure the ability to buy and gain a commitment first every time. In addition to giving yourself the opportunity to make a profit, starting at list will also greatly increase your chances of making a sale. In many cases, customers expect some give and take. Don't limit yourself by eliminating your opportunity. The surest way to a successful career in vehicle sales is to build your credibility with the knowledge of your products and your assessment skills, not your early discounting skills.

FINAL THOUGHT

Presenting the figures should be the easiest step in the sales process, and it can be if you always start and end with your process in mind. Take the time to understand how important your consistency is in this step, and condition yourself to become consistent. When you fully believe in having your presentation become habit and not allowing yourself to stray from your path, you will see how easy it is to prepare yourself and your customers to reach an agreement on your terms.

8

CLOSING THE SALE

The vast majority of customers are looking for a good deal, or one that they deem fair. However, one's definition of a good deal is not a constant. It will vary from customer to customer. A good deal is not a specific number or a defined set of completions. A good deal is the perception of the buyer, and is a result of the value that has been created. It is where the perceived total value of an offering is equal to the investment required.

Making the deal, or closing is everything. It is the result we must achieve before your customers will be able to enjoy the vehicle you and they have selected. However, even with the best presentation of figures, not all of your customers will agree to settle right away. Because of this we must practice closing our customers on agreeable terms. We have to become experienced in successfully persuading our customers and closing the deal.

UNDERSTANDING THE CLOSE

Closing the sale is the act of you and your customers agreeing to the terms of delivery and accepting the figures that have been presented. Closing is not something you just ask for, it is something that you build to throughout the steps. It's where every question you ask and every piece of information you provide will guide and motivate your customers toward purchasing the selected vehicle.

The key to closing is preparing your customers to be closed. It is a careful analysis of their wants and needs and the formulation of the path necessary to persuade them to make a decision. Closing is an art. It's recognizing what your customers are thinking and feeling, and understanding why. It is identifying their motivations and hesitations, and possessing the insight to understand what influences will persuade them. It is recognizing what answers will influence them to maintain, alter, or rethink their current point of view, after you have established their point of view.

Closing is also tying up the loose ends. It's isolating the variables of the deal and gaining acceptance on each before proceeding to the next. When closing, you isolate the vehicle, isolate the objections, and then isolate the figures. A top salesperson will always secure the details before they start to negotiate a figure. This allows them to build to a close on a successful and uninterrupted path.

Closing is additionally knowing when to close. It's knowing their receptivity is high by the telltale signs of their emotions and actions. It is recognizing when the timing is right. It's the point where you have established value in the customer's eyes and they have accepted that they will be purchasing. It is when you can sense they are already planning their lives around their new vehicle.

WHAT CLOSING IS NOT

What closing *is not* is simple. Closing is not just discounting a selected vehicle in the hope that someone might say yes. It is not solely negotiating the price to be paid. It is the balancing of price and value. For the successful salesperson, the start of the price discussion is merely another opportunity to build more value.

CLOSE WITH CONFIDENCE

The first rule in closing is to understand the importance of assuming that your customers will agree to the terms that have been presented. Some customers will close easy, and some will be challenging. To best position yourself for an agreeable response, it is essential that you portray confidence in the figures you have presented. Understand that people are very astute in reading the subconscious language of your mannerisms. They will recognize any insecurity or uncertainty in your beliefs. If your customers see that you believe in the numbers offered, they, too, will be much more likely to believe and ultimately accept them. If they see you are uncomfortable with the numbers, they too will be uncomfortable. Your customers will always be less likely to agree if they feel a better price is possible.

Too many times, a salesperson will give up profit or lose the sale by consciously or subconsciously indicating that a better deal can be had. Once you have a commitment and your customers are sitting down, show confidence in your figures. Always assume that they will accept the figures you present when you start the process.

In sales and in closing, success is in doing the right things and doing them well; and believing in yourself is the basis for this success. The formation of your security is a process much like that of sales itself. It is the result of following your beliefs. If you believe in your vehicles, believe in your dealership, and believe in the level of service you will provide, your security will shine through and give you the confidence needed to succeed. You have to show belief in what you present before others will believe in them as well. Confidence breeds trust, and trust is essential to your customer's acceptance.

IT IS NOT ALWAYS PRICE

Almost all customers will lead you to believe that they only care about one thing. This one thing is price. They want you to believe that their whole decision is based on the bottom line. In fact, experienced shoppers will have inexperienced salespeople jumping through hoops to satisfy all of their price questions and demands. Do not let this happen to you. Take control by adhering to the sequence of the process and build the value in your offering.

When negotiating a deal, be strong in your desire to close the sale and maintain a profit. Take into consideration the time you spent learning about your vehicles and the time and effort spent training yourself. Also, consider the level of service that you will give your customers after the sale. If you were successful in building rapport, let them know the value of having you as a salesperson. Reiterate the quality of the service that you and your dealership will provide. Do not be shy; billions of dollars a year are spent in the service industry. Why should yours be free?

Additionally, do not impose your own feelings on what a good deal is or assume what the customer will or will not pay. Let this characteristic remain in the possession of underperforming salespeople. Your customer's perception of a good deal is one of creation. It is also unique and susceptible to outside influence. In sales, a customer's perception of value is completely proportional to the salesperson's ability to build value. The more value you are able to create the more likely your customer will accept the terms you have presented and purchase your vehicle. This is absolutely true. Value is in the eye of the beholder. This is why there is no unimportant step in this process. Each step is part of a highly coordinated plan to increase the perception of value in your prospect's mind. It is another reason some salespeople will consistently sell more than others. Some salespeople will understand this and believe in building value throughout their process, and some will agree to just talk about the price.

Understand that price is often not the determining factor in a purchase. Look at the clothes you are wearing. Can you honestly say that everything you're wearing was purchased because it was the least expensive stuff you could find? Probably not. In fact, price probably wasn't an issue in many of your items. If you doubt this, try to recall how much you paid for each. If you've had them for any period of time, it will be difficult. The fact is that the average consumer will remember the experience of a purchase far longer than they will remember the price. So think in the future.

START FRESH

In sales there will always be difficult customers. However, do not let these customers determine your pattern of thought. Just because your last was not swayed by your efforts, don't assume your next one won't be either. Learn from your past to help your future, not taint it. All customers may appear challenging when first addressing the purchase price, however, you must believe that not all will continue to be challenging. Do not let yourself fall into the belief, that it's all about the price. It is not. It's only just about price when you choose to let go of your value building process.

ALWAYS ABOUT THE VALUE

The best way to continue the closing process is to start rebuilding value, not to start lowering the price. Every time your customer states they are not sure about the deal or admit they want a lower price, keep building value. Continue to sell yourself, your dealership, and your vehicle. Understand that your customer's perceptions of value only have to equal the expense involved, and this can be accomplished just as easily by increasing their awareness of value as by lowering the price. As long as they are being reasonable, a little extra value-building time will only help.

NEGOTIATING THE FIGURES

Well, okay. Even though you followed the process to build value first and presented your figures with absolute confidence, your customers are still not agreeing. They still aren't going to pay the current market value, and they want more for their trade. On top of that, the down payment is too high. Well, let's get to work. In some cases, despite your best efforts, these factors may not yet be acceptable, and you must now seek to negotiate the figures. Here we go. As usual, we will start at the beginning.

Before we start, let me set the stage. Our process is a guide to follow when negotiating. However, whenever there is more than one party involved in any interaction, there will always be the times that all does not go as planned. In a negotiation, most of your customers will have different levels of desire and skill. Most will have their own methods or angles they choose to use. Meaning, your varied customers will act or respond in varied ways. So, as we go over the outline of our plan, I will pause in the appropriate spaces to offer some advice for customer's most common actions. However, please be sure to see the overall outline of the process as well. Although there is no common blueprint for a customer's input, there is a blueprint on how you should set your path when negotiating.

START AT ALL THE MONEY

When opening with your figures, always start at the list or full retail price. We start at all the money for two reasons. The first, of course, is because they might accept it. The second is because it will leave us someplace to go. Most people, in negotiating, will want some feel of give and take. In fact, many customers think of the close as a series of give and take. If you have a commitment, leave yourself room.

PLAY IT SLOW

Once you have opened up the deal, and your customers don't initially accept, do not immediately counteroffer your offer or look for a counteroffer before spending some time justifying the figures you've presented. If you quickly or randomly discount your own numbers, the customer will expect you to do so over and over again. This will leave you with no credibility and will afford them control in the negotiation.

Also, it is not yet time to ask or even allow a quick counteroffer. You do not want them to initiate a counteroffer unless you have had the time to analyze that it would likely be close. It might be too much, too fast. They might think of your initial numbers as too high and counter with figures that are too low. If they do give an offer, don't even acknowledge it, just refuse to hear it. Your customers will usually use their first spoken offer, no matter how low it may be, as a basis for where they eventually want to be. This difference may be too much to overcome. At this early point, you want to continue building your rapport and value until they agree, or at least until you feel confident that their offer will be close to acceptable. You want to avoid creating a spoken reference for them to have to compare with later on, creating an uphill battle throughout the close.

You always want to set the first number and always want to set the first counter if one is needed. If you determine that your customer's acceptance is not forthcoming, it is still you who will want to initiate the next step. This is to keep the first spoken amount of difference in your control. Rather than pursuing a potentially risky counteroffer, you want to make the first attempt to refigure your variable. The reasoning behind this is simple. Most people want to keep their credibility. Any alteration from their offered number may be seen as losing face. If a certain style of buyer was to give a return number, they may actually feel that they would be losing credibility if they altered too much. Some people's personalities don't allow them to lose face. Some will feel that altering their position is a sign of personal weakness. I have actually seen people walk away from a deal that they really wanted because their pride would not let them accept it. Do not put yourself in this position.

ADJUSTING OUR OFFER

When negotiating the actual figures, remember it is our intention to keep all but one of the figures on our worksheet a constant. We want to direct the focus to the figure of most contention. We do not want to negotiate in one part of the equation only to have to re-negotiate in the next. In addition, focusing on one figure will create less resistance to an agreement on their lesser concerns because they will still have the opportunity to adjust the movement of the remaining figure. They will not have the anxiety involved in moving forward when agreeing to variables of lesser contention because these issues will not be the final points of agreement. Focusing on one specific parameter is what we helped prepare for by separating the variables and steering their attention to a specific one when presenting the figures. Once you have successfully isolated your focus and reconfirmed their commitment, you want to test their price resolve in a cautious manner. It is here that you will initiate your next move. The key to successful negotiating is to start with small increments in a questioning approach. In addition to wanting to set the first figures, again, you want to set the first counteroffer.

You want to minimally adjust your separated figure of most concern in the direction of their favor. When this point arrives, ask your customers if moving the figure a hundred or two would help persuade them to move forward. This method of negotiating gives you the opportunity to make more profit, build credibility with your first offer, and allows further room to move. Note: Always remain silent after asking a closing question. Your silence will help yield their response.

If a hundred or two more won't do it, it still may or may not be safe to solicit an offer from them. If you are able to sense from their expressions or mannerisms that their offer is likely to be close to your original figure, allow them to voice their offer. If not, continue building your value, publicly encouraging them to keep their offer close or to not make an offer at all.

RAISE YOUR OBSERVATION

If your efforts do solicit an offer, and you feel it is still lower than they will eventually agree to, question if they have information to support their offer. Ask yourself if they are just going by feel. Many times, customers will voice a price objection, disagreement, or a low counteroffer simply because that is what they have coached themselves to do. Additionally, in many instances, they may be testing your reaction for a measure of what they should request. At this stage, you will often have to raise your level of observation and people-reading skills to determine the direction they are leaning. You will have to assess and analyze their resolve. You will have to be intuitive and creative in determining and responding to the actions and reactions that occur.

If they reveal an unreasonable offer, interrupt their request or again refuse to acknowledge it. If you do not react immediately in the negative to an unreasonable offer, they may consider their offer acceptable, or close to acceptable. If it is not, be quick to dismiss it. Relay to them that their offer is completely unacceptable. Do not give them any impression that it is remotely agreeable. It is the same reasoning here as with not agreeing to hear their earlier, quick-response offer. If you are not close, avoid this common mistake, and do not act like you are. This is very important and worth repeating. Please think this out. Do not write this offer down, take it to your manager, or even repeat it out loud. You in no way want to show any validation of an unacceptable offer, or you will likely never be able to revalue their perception of a more reasonable offer. If your customer sees any acceptance of their offer, trust me, they will stick like glue to it and you probably won't be able to sell them a car. Always move for a more reasonable offer up front, or you may never be able to work them up. Gauge their level of closeness with each exchange and constantly analyze any change in their thinking before acknowledging their response. Include some value-building and rapport-building time here again.

QUESTION THE EVIDENCE

If your customers state that your figures are too high, ask, "Why do you say that?" They might realize that they have no basis for their statements. They may realize that they have no relevant information to support their claim or initiate a lower counteroffer. If they do offer information, such as another dealer, validate the information. Verify that what you are comparing is the same. Further, if their information is comparable, there is no law that says you have to be cheaper. Remember, the quality of you and your dealership's service is a remaining variable and one that should set you apart.

While you continue to investigate your customer's resolve, continue to solicit a reasonable counteroffer. Eventually, most of your customers will come around. Remember, due to the level of rapport and service that you've created earlier in your interaction, they will often look for reasons to agree.

TRY ONCE AGAIN

If you feel you're getting close, try one more time to offer another hundred or two off and gain their acceptance. This second re-offer is another reason to avoid hearing any offer that is too low, because if they sense that you acknowledged their low offer, they may become insulted or defensive by your small move. However, if you work with a clean and untainted slate, they'll be more likely to see your response as something more within reason. Once you restate your offer, again seek their acceptance.

NOW SEEK THE OFFER

If again the customer does not close, you must now abandon your discounting approach and become persistent in your efforts to seek an acceptable offer. You want to limit the number of moves in their direction. You do not want to negotiate against yourself. If they see your moves developing a pattern, they will remain in their current position and let you continue. You have to involve them. At this point, you have to concentrate on soliciting an offer from them and then seek to close on the difference.

CLOSING IS PERSISTENCE

The easiest way to continue closing is with your leading questions. Close from the customer's point of view. Stop and re-ask the questions that will remind them of how they reached this point. Allow them to remember why they agreed to purchase this vehicle. Keep steady in your efforts to close the deal.

Ask the questions that will help restart the flow of their yes answers again, "Mr. Customer, you did say that this was the vehicle and options you wanted, correct?"

"This is your color of choice, right?"

"You are able to make a decision today, aren't you?"

"Well, okay, that being said, at what figures would you be willing to take the vehicle home?" When the negotiations stall, the best action you can take is to repeat your various confirming questions, continue to build value in yourself, your dealership, and the vehicle, and then solicit an offer. Be polite and courteous, but be persistent. You must push for a figure in which they will do business.

When encouraging your customer's offer, use your radar to help steer them to the answers you want. Yes, be quiet when you ask a closing question, but at the instant you see their answer is not the one you want, speak up. Ask another confirming question, and then re-ask your closing question. Learn to foresee the words they are about to speak by observing and analyzing the physical movements leading up to their delivery.

When asking your confirming questions, go for the yeses. Sometimes, when seeking to start momentum, you may have to go for the easy yeses just to get the ownership mood restarted. Remember, a customer's yes-saying mood is important. It is a law of human nature to remain on the same path unless acted upon. In some cases, you might have to start further back in your history or ask the obvious to get your first yes. For example, "Sir, you did wake up this morning, correct?"

Okay, maybe not that far back, but go back as far as necessary to get a positive response. "Sir, you did come here to search for a car, didn't you?"

Sometimes, if your customers cease negotiating because they become frustrated or just feel they aren't close, you may actually have to go lower than you want to or even can just to interest them again. Although you want to avoid doing this if at all possible, it may be necessary to jumpstart a stalled negotiation. You cannot build on a no. You can only build on a yes, so keep trying.

CONTINUE FROM THE CUSTOMER'S POSITION

When closing, you want to think like your buyers. When you reach this point in your negotiation, pause, and put yourself in their position. Seriously, just stop for a second and think. Try to look at the negotiation from their point of view. Try to envision what they are thinking. Analyze what they are saying with their words versus what they're saying with their manner. Use the feedback you are receiving to gauge your customer's level of commitment. Watch to see if their physical language and facial expressions line up. Do they want to own the car? How much do they want to own the car? Are they negotiating to determine if they will own or have they already decided on ownership and are just negotiating for price? When negotiating, always ask yourself if they will close at these figures. Are you leaving money on the table?

Their words may say discount, but their actions may say they will purchase at or near the figure requested. At this stage, you have to be able to read your customers and adjust your approach. Depending on the personalities of your customers or their negotiating stance, it may be better to quicken your pace with a fast repetition of small increments or slow it down with some small talk. Compare their resolve to own the selected vehicle against their resolve in getting a discount.

Do not give up profit if it is not necessary. Analyze where you are and determine your most beneficial approach.

EVALUATE THEIR OFFER

When you are able to solicit their most reasonable counteroffer, take a second to look at it. Write it down on your worksheet and then pause. Look at it as if to study its acceptability. Learn to control your emotions and expressions. It's here that your customers will often base their next move, according to your reaction. If you jump up and do the victory dance, they might try to take back their offer. Your reaction should be based on the degree of discount their offer represents. Your response should range from, "Hmm, let me see if I can get this approved," to, "I can't accept that offer."

Depending on the degree of acceptability, it may still be best here to talk them up to a higher offer, or you could just take it to your manger for approval. This, of course, depends on the feel of the negotiation. Sometimes the tension or anxiety in a negotiation should be relieved. If you determine that their offer is reasonable or your negotiation warrants a break, take their offer to the manager's desk and let them know that you will work to make a deal happen.

Note: I do not believe in having customers sign the offer or give a deposit at this stage in most cases. Working off trust will produce less anxiety. If your customers are going to back out of their offer, their signature or deposit means nothing anyway, so why add to the apprehension? By the way, never say, "sign here" or, "I need your signature." Have them, "authorize the paperwork."

Now, sometimes, if your customer's anxiety level is low or they are of the hard-to-tie-down nature, a little extra confirmation may help. Unfortunately, there is no best method. You have to play it by feel. Again, you have to be able to observe and analyze your customer's thoughts.

ANOTHER COUNTEROFFER

Sometimes, again depending on the nature of your negotiation or the acceptability of the customer's offer, you may choose to either accept their offer or counter it. Here as well, this all must be played by feel. For example, if you do not counter their offer, your customers may feel they offered too much and re-weigh their offer. At other times however, they might just explode from the perceived hassle and run for the door. There is no set right answer. In this circumstance, you have to assess your customers intently and accurately. Get all you can, but don't overdo it.

AUTHENTICATE YOUR COUNTEROFFER

When you or your manager is preparing a counteroffer, always use exact-looking numbers. Perception is still what matters most. Exact numbers like this sound more believable as a good deal, one based on a tight level of acceptability, where effort and multiple calculations were involved. Let them know that you are trying to save them every expense possible. Note that if you feel that the exchange of offers will necessitate more than one trip, save this method for what you hope will be your last trip. This way, it won't lose its effect for the final close.

BE EXCITED ABOUT YOUR OFFER

When you come back with the counteroffer, let your customers know you have some great news. Let them know that you have a great deal for them and that you're excited for them. Let them know that they are just one step away from owning their new car. Give them the figures, and without pause, ask for their agreement.

Move to strike a deal here. Move at a fast pace if not quickly accepted. Seek to narrow the gap with a small series of give and take. Time at this point is usually not to be wasted. Have your manager give you a little room for negotiation, if needed. Reaching a deal at this stage is nothing more than a series of small compromises. Be persistent. Seek to move quickly beyond any objections they may have and get their agreement.

SHARE THE EXCITEMENT

If your manager is a good closer, now may be a good time for a turnover if a deal still can't be reached. If your manager is available, introduce him or her and leave. Stay close enough to be there if called, but not close enough to be involved. You want to leave because you want to allow your customers to make a new decision. Remember, your customers will be less likely to change their minds and say yes in front of you because they will have to lose their own sense of credibility if they accept the agreement as it stands. So, stay in hearing distance, but stay out of view.

If your manager was unable to close them, try some more on your own. Managers are usually good closers, and they may have softened your customers up for your reattempt. Your friendly face may be all they need to move forward with a deal. If they close here, congratulations. If not, don't worry, we are not done yet. There is more to come in the following chapters.

THE FINAL THOUGHT

The closing process is really very simple. Reaffirm your customer's selection, reaffirm the value, present new information to satisfy their objections, and ask again for the sale. Successfully closing a tough sale is the result of having the ability to repeat the closing process, all while maintaining your customer's willingness to remain participants.

Whenever I am closing a tough sale, I think about the directions I get for things that say, "Complete this step and repeat."

Every time you offer new information to your customer about why they should close, or are able to reestablish their perception of value, ask again for the sale. Repeat the step. Remember, when customer says no, they are only saying no as a result of the information they presently have. If you are able to offer them new information, you should not be shy in asking them to make a new decision. This new information may be more value, an additional option, or even sometimes a lower price.

Whatever it is, have the desire and persistence to find out. Then have the desire and persistence to keep trying to satisfy these hesitations and successfully complete the sale. Be a good salesperson. Let your customer start enjoying their new vehicle right away.

9

MY FAVORITE CLOSES

A close is when the terms of a deal are stated and an agreement is being reached. It is when you attempt to lay the final groundwork for your concluding goal. In sales, there are lots of set plans or methods that will help transition our customers smoothly from buyers to owners. Within each step of our sales process, we will often have to close our customers on one parameter or another in order for them to move to the next. Within each step are often a series of mini-closes that all lead up to the final, most important one, the purchase. I have listed my favorite closes here.

For this list of closes, I have tried to use the most recognized title for each and explain them in simple terms. This is to help you identify with each one when the appropriate time or opportunity presents itself. When reading through them, try to envision how and where you may use them for the progression of each step and the final agreement. I have also included in each some advice to help you get a better feel for when and where each will be of use. Please, feel free to adjust your presentation of each as it may relate to your customer's style, the style of your delivery, or where in the process they may be of most benefit.

Okay, here we go. But before we get started, I want to make one major point: persistence. When closing, persistence is essential. Make as many attempts to close as your customers will let you. Use every one of the closes listed here, and more if necessary. Okay, now we're ready.

ASSUMPTION CLOSE: If you completed all the steps in the process and created a desire, this is the easiest one to close with. After you state your proposal, continue writing up the purchase order. Just assume they are ready to buy. A good lead to this close, immediately following the presentation of your figures, might be to say, "Okay, then, how were you going to be titling the vehicle, in your name only or with your wife as well?" When your customer responds, consider the deal closed. Just write it up. This close is that simple. In this example, we even made it easier for them to respond, by supplying their choice of answers.

INVITATION CLOSE: This is where you simply invite your customer to take the deal. It might go like this, "Well, what do you think? Would you like to give it a try?" Simple and straightforward. If they say okay write it up. If they say no, ask why not, then handle the objection. When you do overcome the objection, invite them again.

SECONDARY QUESTION CLOSE: This is where you would present two questions at once. The first of which will confirm the sale; the second is where the answer will give information to initiate the transaction. Note the second question is something that is easy to respond to and that is what we want.

It is human nature for a person to respond to the last or easiest question first. When your customers respond positively to the second question, they have essentially agreed with your first question, right? It may go like this, "Okay, at this point, all we have to do is decide when would be a good time for you to pick up your new car." and continue right away with, "Do you have a copy of your license handy for the paperwork?" Then, casually extend your hand to receive their license. When they hand you their license, use it to start writing up the order. They have agreed to take delivery. Continue with your paperwork and involve them. Don't worry about an answer to the first question, because it's not specific to actually making a deal. Just keep moving forward, knowing that it will likely fall into place as you continue

This close is actually assuming the sale without being too direct. With this close, as with any form of assumption close, it is imperative to keep the customer busy. Remember to give them something to do immediately upon the positive response to your second question. Have them fill out a form or two. If you ask for an insurance card and they don't have one, move on and offer another task. Start them with a credit application or even the purchase order if they are paying cash. Do not risk letting the customer go out to their trade to retrieve anything just yet, or letting them have any alone time at all. It is a very delicate time between when they agree and when they go into the business office. Any idle time here, and your deal will be at risk.

AGREEABLE CLOSE: This is where you simply ask, "Mr. Customer, does all of this sound agreeable to you?" If he says yes, proceed with, "Okay, all that's left now is a little paperwork." Start writing it up.

This close is a combination of the invitation and the assumption close. I like this close because it is one that most people want to respond to positively. Many people have a built-in sense that being agreeable is the acceptable way to interact.

Note: Have your paperwork procedure down pat. Proceed with no change in emotion and carry on an idle conversation while completing paperwork. Act as if this is just the next step. If your temperament changes, you may make your customers uneasy. Do not bring attention to their implied acceptance. Just proceed like you expected their positive answer, and never look back.

IF-THE-PAYMENTS-WORK CLOSE: This close should always be the next attempt to keep their forward progress going if they do not initially agree to the terms and if they are financing. To help with this close, indicate that what really matters is the payment and that they should determine that before they consider acceptance. Persuade them to make their decision based on the terms of the payment. It may go like this, "Okay, sir, let me ask you a question. If we can somehow adjust these figures and work out the financial terms to where your monthly payment is acceptable," pause here, "is this a vehicle you would want to own?" If they say yes, simply write it up.

Oh, and remember, you did not discuss a discount, so write it up at list and have the manager okay for finance. If the deal has to be adjusted a little to fit into the customer's parameters, that's okay. It is still better to write it at list and try. If you don't try, you won't get. This is the close you would like to have made available by leaving the payment undetermined while presenting the figures. You want to balance your information to maintain interest and curiosity. This close is simply the easiest way to have your financing customers proceed to the finance office, and this is the forward direction you want.

ANSWER-THE-FINAL-OBJECTION CLOSE: This is where you would have your customer agree to a deal on the idea that moving forward is contingent upon resolving one last variable. This is a transition close. It can be used at any stage of the process. You steer the close and forward momentum to one last objection, and then isolate it as the customer's last point of contention. This may be price related, such as when negotiating the figures, or could be any other parameter of the deal. When negotiating, it might go like this, "Okay, Mr. Buyer, so what you're saying is that if I can agree to your last request of $. . . on the trade and keep all of the other figures as presented, we can write up the paperwork, right?"

Get your customer's commitment before you give them yours. Remember, like the payment close, this is also a close you should set up when presenting the figures, in case you have to negotiate. Another example of this close for an earlier step in your sales process may go like this, "Let me ask you a question." Pause. "If I could find an open parking lot with little or no traffic, you would want to take a small test drive, am I right?" Seek to determine your customer's objection and then lead them to overcome it. For the first example, when negotiating the figures, you might not know if you can accomplish their last request. That is still okay. Your goal here is to get a commitment off which you can work. Also, this will help put them in a yes-saying mood. It will give them the feeling, and sometimes relief, that ownership is accepted. Once people commit to a deal, they are much more likely to be flexible

94

to ensure that they keep the feeling of acceptance. If it's reasonable and you can accomplish it, do it. If you cannot meet their requests, counter with your own offer. When closing, always seek to work off the customer's commitments.

SUMMARY CLOSE: Here, you will seek to sum up all the variables for the customer and ask for the deal. Tying up the loose ends will help both you and them feel good about moving forward. An example for negotiating might be, "Okay, so what you're saying is that if I can get your payment to $400 per month with $500 down, pay off your trade, and repair that scratch, we have a deal, right?"

Again, you are seeking a commitment that you can build upon. Once you have a commitment, continue forward. Note: With regards to the summary above, where the payment has been settled and summarized, just say okay upon the customer's acceptance and start to write it up. Being the salesperson, you do not have access to the payment screen. This is fine. You have not committed, they have. Your job is done. Here is where you say, "Okay, great. Let's write it up and give it to the business office for the monthly numbers." That's it. Start writing. Don't try to tackle everything at once. Let things proceed one step at a time. Remember, your intention as a salesperson is to facilitate your customer's move into the finance office. You should never assume what your customers will or won't agree to in that office. Remember, the business managers are generally the strongest closers in the dealership. They are a fresh face for your customer and are skilled at going the last fifteen yards. To the point, if you get this type of commitment, write it up, have the manager sign it, and give it to finance.

NO-MONEY-DOWN CLOSE: Just as it sounds, "Okay, then, what you're telling me is that if I can get you approved with no money down, you will take the car, correct?" That's it. When they agree, write it up.

Note that you should always encourage your customer's acceptance by slightly nodding your head with an expression of approval when you are closing to get a positive response. Also note that you do not necessarily have to know if you can accomplish this. At this point, you are confirming their request and the close. This keeps the negotiation open and gets the customer in a yes-saying groove.

This close is another example of the importance of the yes saying pattern. Keep in mind that it is essential to stay away from questions that will produce a no, and it's just as important to continue with questions that will produce a yes. Make no mistake; the little yeses will lead to the big yes. This is what momentum is all about. Also remember that sometimes, if they are in a no-saying groove, you may have to dip below where you would want to or even can be, just to get them to start with the little yeses. Using the premise of if, will build on what you have. In most cases, it is far easier to bump customers on a yes than to change their direction from a no.

LET'S-PROCEED-ANYWAY CLOSE: Don't laugh. This one has worked for me many times. This is where you simply cannot come to an agreement. You might set this close up like this, "Mr. Customer, you want this deal to work, right? Well, I do, too. So, let's continue writing up the order, and I'm sure we will get something worked out. Okay?"

This does three things. One, it gets customers in the yes-saying groove. Two, it involves them with more of an investment. And third, since you are completing the paperwork, there will be little time for them to change their minds when they do say yes. Note: Any opportunity you have to increase the customer's investment in either time or information will usually work in your favor if your customers are close to agreeing. As long as they are still sitting in front of you, you have the green light to keep closing.

BEN FRANKLIN CLOSE: This is a great close for the indecisive customer. It is where you draw a line down the center of a blank sheet of paper. You then list all the positive reasons to do the deal on the left and all the reasons not to on the right. Help them with the reasons they should do the deal, and then help with the reasons not to do the deal. When this is completed, count up the reasons and ask for the sale.

Note, being that this close is very well known, some customers may see it as a technique. If this is the case, just agree with them. If they recognize it, admire their perception, and admit that yes, it is. However, let them know that the reason it's so popular is because it makes good sense. Let them know that many wise decisions were made as a result of this analysis. Once they agree, help them get started.

NOT-FOREVER CLOSE: I like this close. It helps relieve the pressure by putting things in perspective. When they can afford it and their acceptance is near, let them know that this probably won't be their last car. Just say, "This won't be your last car right? Okay, then try it for a while."

When you are in the late stages of a close, sometimes people are just afraid of making a mistake. They feel that making a decision will limit future options. Let them know that this is not a lifelong decision, "Go ahead and give it a try. You will have plenty of opportunities to make other, more important decisions down the road. Let's get past this one so you can get on with the more important things in your life."

This close may sound kind of far-fetched, but I have seen people agree almost immediately upon presenting this. Lots. If you think about it, it really does put things in perspective. It relieves the pressure by taking the importance off the decision.

If your customers are still unsure after you've attempted this or any close, pause for a minute and try some of the confirming questions you learned about earlier. An example may be, "You did say your wife liked the sunroof and that your kids will be excited about the DVD, right? Okay, let's go ahead. You deserve it."

Remember that a series of these will help to create your momentum. Note that with this example, you are taking it back to an emotional decision and involving other people. You're providing an image for your customers of enjoying the benefits of ownership. Close on their impending shared enjoyment, not the price. As you use this close, or any other listed in this chapter, always be sure to use the time between your efforts to help set up and encourage your customer's approval for your next attempt.

EMPLOYEE CLOSE: In most dealerships, there will usually be another person you work with who either owns or drives a vehicle comparable to the one you are showing. When you have customers who need a little extra encouragement, introduce them to this person for a testimonial on why they chose their vehicle and how it has been for them. This is a strong second opinion. Your customers know that in most cases, an employee of a dealership is usually a car person and wouldn't choose a vehicle that was not deemed a good choice. This employee may be a service writer, a mechanic, or even another salesman. The word of another who presently owns or has chosen to drive a vehicle that your customers are currently considering is often the affirmation they want before moving forward.

FREE-STUFF CLOSE: Offer to give your customer something if they agree to the deal. Offer or agree to include mats, a pin stripe, a tank of gas, a free oil change, a future detail, a trailer hitch, or whatever. Find their hot button. Use your memory and think of something they may have mentioned earlier.

This is probably one of the more common closes and one customers will often look for. It's quite often effective, and in many cases, is the final piece of the deal. Just remember to leverage a commitment as a condition to receiving the stuff. It might go like this, "If I can throw in some free floor mats, we have a deal, right?" This close is also one more reason to start the negotiation with all the money. Leave yourself some room.

BOTH-SIDES CLOSE: This close is where you present and argue both sides of the decision at hand. This is my favorite close for when the customer is ready, yet just a little indecisive. This can be for when your customers are deciding between vehicles, financial options, or even on whether to agree to a deal or not. It's where you represent both the positives and negatives of each option in a discussion where you ultimately sway your customers to their best choice by presenting one side more eloquently than the other.

The key to this close is to place yourself empathetically in their position and verbally balance the options from their point of view to help move them to a decision. It is to both have and show concern, and therefore have influence with your guidance. This close is always best presented in a discussion with the restating of the known facts of each, while involving and encouraging your customer's input with your questions. This close makes you a consultative salesperson. It builds your credibility with both the argument you present and the understanding of the pros and cons of each side. It also demonstrates that you care enough about the decision and your customer's best interest to help them see both the pluses and minuses. It is like having a debate in which your customers are both participants and audience. It's like the Ben Franklin close without the paper and with more open involvement.

I agree that this close takes a great deal of understanding of both your customer's motivating factors and the facts of the decision, but is very effective if you are observant, creative, and forward thinking. A good example of this close would be when you are deciding between the different options while selecting a vehicle. Learn where they may be or should be leaning with your discovery-and-need assessment questions and then help them realize it with your leading questions. If done properly, this might be one of the best closes for the customer who is on the verge or indecisive.

This close is so effective because, as in most difficult decisions, your customers will internally weigh their decisions anyway. What this close does is allow you to enter and become part of their internal decision-making process. It brings the customer's thought-process out in the open, where you will be better able to understand and ultimately help them move to a decision. This is by far my most trusted and successful standby close for when the more assumptive closes fail to initiate a forward move. Take the time to envision this close, realize its effectiveness, and practice it with your upcoming decisions.

AVAILABLE CLOSE: At some time in their past, most people have wanted something that was unavailable. The item may have been sold out, not yet built, on back order, at another location, or limited in how many were available. This close is simply to inquire, "If the vehicle that you have requested was available, would you be interested in owning it today?"

This close will work in most stages of the process and its directness can be adjusted to fit your customers and the situation. Another example for earlier in the process might be, "If the alloy wheels were available with the sport package, is that something that you would prefer?" This close offers both a commitment and a move forward.

SWITCH-CAR CLOSE: This one should be reserved for when several previous attempts to close have failed. Basically, you sigh, sit back, and say, "Mr. Customer, it just doesn't look like the figures are going to work on this car. Maybe we should step down to another model."

If the customer says, "No, this is the car I want," keep on closing. He has just furthered himself toward a commitment. If he says, "Okay," then show him another vehicle. He might like it, or he might bump himself on price and switch back to the first. This will, in either case, validate your figures as being the best possible deal. Sometimes all people want is a sign that they are getting a good deal.

TAKEAWAY CLOSE: This close is a little risky and only recommended for customers with certain demeanors. Basically, this is reverse thinking and will work best with non-agreeable or opposite type thinkers. This close is based on the same premise as the available close, only in reverse. This technique will challenge their ego. Take the car or deal away, and they might want it more. It may go like this, "Maybe this just isn't the right truck for you, besides, I think another salesperson has a customer interested in it anyway." Now remain silent. Odds are they will open the possibilities back up.

To help you understand this approach, picture two kids in the sandbox. One is playing happily with his toy crane and loader and paying no attention to his truck. However, let his friend come close to the truck, and watch the fight ensue. Many people never outgrow this way of thinking. Many of your customers will develop a newfound want if they feel they no longer have access to their selected vehicle. They might not miss it until it's off the bargaining table. It may also be a pressure release for customers who are stalled by anxiety. No longer having an impending decision may actually release their tension and allow them to move forward.

REDUCE-THE-EXPENSE CLOSE: This, like the Ben Franklin close, is also a very well known and commonly offered close. Here too, if they see it as a technique, admit it. Just say, "Okay, but it makes sense, right?" Let's take a look.

This is for the customer who states that your bottom line or figure of contention is higher than they would like. For this close, simply take the difference between where your numbers are and where they want them to be, and spread it out over time. Reduce it to an inconsequential amount. For example, if you are at $14,000 for the customer's selected vehicle and they want to be at $12,500, you have an established difference of $1500. Ask them how long they plan to keep the car and add a little time for safe measure. For argument's sake, say they will keep it for five years. That is the same as $300 a year or about $25 per month. So, your final step of this close may be, "Sir, the difference is less than a dollar a day. You wouldn't let pennies a day stop you from owning the car you wanted, would you?" Pause and give your of-course-not look.

If the customer says no, write it up. If he says yes, appeal to his sense of reason. Let him know that this minimal amount is not a valid reason for not moving forward. Ask if pennies a day will affect his budget. If he says no, write it up. If he says yes, verify it. Then ask him again. As you may realize by now, this may not be the real reason. He may be working you for every nickel, or he may be unsure about something other than price. If you suspect the first, maintain your course and appeal to his sense of reason or fair play. If you have good rapport and he can afford it, tell him to stop being so cheap while you smile or laugh. This might break the ice and complete the sale. If, however, he is unsure about something else, continue to search for his objection. A good test here would be to ask, "Okay, look, we know it's not the money, so what is it? What is holding you up from enjoying your new vehicle?" From here, just pause. Pressure him for a response with your silence. Then take his answer and proceed to overcome his objection. Oh, up next: Objections.

TAKE IT HOME CLOSE: This close is usually left for the manager and should be offered when most nothing else works. This is because you want to do all you can to wrap it up and lock in a today signed deal first. But make no mistake; this is a very effective close to follow up with if a deal cannot be initially reached. Let the customer take the vehicle home, even without a commitment, if necessary. This is done in the hope that they'll fall in love with it. Most of the time, they will. If you are able to get your customer to take their selected vehicle home, the odds are overwhelmingly in your favor. Convince them to take the vehicle if you have to. Agree with them that this is an important decision and they should do all they can to make sure it is the right vehicle. If they are hesitant, try asking, "Did you try that shirt on before you bought it?" They will probably respond positively. When they do, your response should be, "If you tried on a $20 investment for comfort, wouldn't it make sense to make sure you were comfortable with a $20,000 investment?" Pause here and give them your look-of-yes. Persuade them.

Another suggestion for this close is to have them to agree to do all the paperwork now, still with no obligation, to lock in today's offer. Just state that if they choose not to take the car for any reason, you will not activate the paperwork. Be persuasive here. Stress that this is good for them because they will have the feeling of ownership without the risk. Let them know that this is the ultimate test-drive. For most, vehicle shopping is stressful. This will give your customer the feeling that their work is over and yet eliminate the anxiety of a permanent decision. Plus, if they take it home, you have other factors on your side. You can bet your customer had an I-got-me-a-new-car grin on their face when they waved to their neighbor that evening. They won't want to do the same wave in their old car. Here again, status is a powerful emotion. Work their emotions.

OKAY-I-GIVE-UP CLOSE: No, we're not really giving up. We are just acting like it to relieve the pressure. Since it might just be the stress that is keeping the customer from saying yes, take the pressure away. First, admit that maybe this deal is not meant to be. Resign yourself to the fact that the terms are just not lining up. Apologize that you were unable to put a deal together. Take the deal completely off the table. Then let the pressure fade. Let the subject change to something other than the deal. Talk about the fact that at least you tried. Agree that there are no hard feelings, and that at the least, you will keep in touch. Note that it is very important to portray having completely given up on trying to put a deal together.

Now, once you are absolutely sure that they believe they will not be making a deal, it's time to put your plan into action. Pause with your most curious look and say, "Sir, just out of curiosity, if there was one parameter of this deal that you could have changed, what would that have been?"

If he responds at all, it's back on. Work it from there. Search for the solution. If the customer is not able to come up with one, or this new angle leads to a dead-end as well, it's time to do what all good closers do. Jump up with enthusiasm and say, "Wait one minute, sir." Then go get a better closer.

FINAL NOTE

Picture a chess player carefully making move after move or a mathematician using various formulas over and over until both sides of an equation adds up. Now ask yourself, how often does a chess player accomplish victory with one or two moves?

Skilled closers deliberate in the same manner as those who solve problems. They visualize the result as fact and seek only to adjust the means that will end in an agreement. They analyze and attempt many courses of action all with one goal in mind, allowing their customers to start enjoying their new vehicles immediately. Much as with the chess player or mathematician, salespeople often have to accomplish their goal through creativity and persistence. They have to understand their customer's needs, be intuitive in finding the best solution, and be creative in their path of acceptance. When closing, understand and believe that most customers will eventually accept your advice, if presented properly, because they want to. They are there for a reason. Accept that you are the expert, allow your advice to persuade, and have the confidence that it will. Refuse to let your customers or yourself down.

During the closing stages of each step, think of yourself as a consultative technician who only acts and reacts with precision, steering your customers to the close with each reconfirming action, question, and response. Lead them to the sale. If you have followed the steps and committed your time and knowledge to helping your customer find the best vehicle for them, search for and define the creativity and persistence to follow through. Help your customers get the new vehicle they really want. Okay? Good! Let's continue, and look at understanding and overcoming some of the likely objections our customers will have.

10

OVERCOME OBJECTIONS

Proper objection handling and the ability to move forward is essential in becoming a top salesperson. There is the probability of customer objections in every part of the process, and these objections will have to be handled in order to proceed.

Understand that in many cases, an objection should be welcomed. Without some form of objection, your customer may not be seriously interested in purchasing a car. In fact, small objections on a specific vehicle or deal will often be the first signs of a persons interest. It is here we must encourage their interest, not discourage it by accepting it as a lack of interest.

In learning to overcome objections, we must first analyze the different aspects of the objection. We must be able to understand why the objection occurred, its true purpose, and its degree of importance. Only then can we go about deciding the best answer for each of the questions or hesitations our customers may have.

WHY THE OBJECTION OCCURRED

An objection is basically an obstacle that your customers will present to not move forward under the present terms or conditions. These obstacles may be derived from one of two possible scenarios. One is where they have realized something is not lining up with their goals, and the other is where they have manufactured a concern to create leverage for their position. Meaning, in some cases your customers will realize their obstacle and in others they may fabricate. Before you are able to respond in an effective manner, you have to determine their motive. You have to be able to recognize whether their objection is a true concern or just a diversion.

An objection that is realized is one where your customers have noticed that some parameter of the vehicle or deal does not conform to their wants or needs. For example, the seating capacity of the vehicle you are showing them won't accommodate the size of their family, or the monthly payments do not fall within their budget.

An objection that's been fabricated is one that your customer's feel will somehow aid them in what they seek to accomplish. An example may be introducing a concern to better negotiate a discount. Here, they may look to point out the vehicle they are looking at has some extra miles on it. And well yes, the car may have some extra miles, but this may just be their request for possible future concessions. They may want a discount.

Whether their objections are real or fabricated, these obstacles will be placed in front of you and will stop or slow your path to the sale. Each of these objections will have a different level of importance, and each of these will have to be analyzed for their true purpose before you decide how to proceed.

THE OBJECTION'S TRUE PURPOSE

When analyzing your customer's objections, think about whether they make sense. Look at their expressions, their actions and their voice to help determine any motive. Try to anticipate the reaction they want you to have and realize what this may accomplish for them. The hurdle we face in our determination is that any objection could be the product of any of the motives stated here or more, so each must be examined uniquely.

In the initial part of the process, you might encounter what appear to be lots of small objections, when in fact; they are actually small, defensive reactions. They are simply insertions meant to either slow things down or give your customers an escape route. Note that these

106

objections are not based on the parameters of the sale or the features of the vehicle. They are only presented as a possible diversion. To help understand the veracity of this, ask yourself: How many times has a customer stated that they have ten minutes to spend only to leave two hours later in their new car? Similar objections will often continue through out the sale; and these you must recognize as a tool, not a lack of interest. However, if they come back and state that it doesn't fit in their garage and they have no street parking, you want to move on and show them another model.

Understand that there are minor and major objections in sales. Listen to the objection being raised. When an objection cannot be overcome, it's not an objection. It is a circumstance or a condition. At this point, you must change directions. You must be able to differentiate your customer's objections and this is always best accomplished by understanding your customer's true purpose.

Additional objections may occur because you still have not established a desire or motive to do business now. Your customers may feel that although there's nothing stopping them from buying, there is not enough reason established that they should. It is here that your customers will likely say they want to think about it or are just not sure. When this pause occurs in the presentation stage, you may try to focus on increasing your customer's desire. When this pause occurs during the close, you may want to stop, reconfirm their selection, and rebuild their feeling of value.

In some cases, your customers may seek to hide their true reasons to avoid them from surfacing. For the objections that appear in disguise, you will have to search a little more thoroughly for their true purpose. For example, the gentleman with whom you are speaking may be slightly embarrassed that it's really his wife who makes all the decisions, or he may not yet have the money he said he had for the down payment. Note that this objection may initially be voiced as the first thing he could think of as a reason not to move forward. Some customers will even put some effort into their objections by trying to come up with something that would be hard to overcome or disagree with. However, if you question each objection as you should, you might uncover their true reasons and overcome them easily. For this example, you may be able to call your customer's wife, or he may not need to put any money down.

Understand there may be an ulterior motive behind each objection you hear, and in each case, you will have to investigate before continuing. These are the objections that you will have to search, pry, and sometimes even twist for before you can attempt to solve them. You must not be shy in asking the questions that will help uncover what is really holding them up. In any case, there is one thing for certain: If you do not know or understand the real reason for the objection, you will never be able to move forward.

When an objection is a diversion, treat it as so and lead them to the sale. When it is a concern, seek to overcome it with new information. When it is a concern that cannot be overcome, seek to find a new direction.

THE DEGREE OF IMPORTANCE

Giving credence to something of little or no concern will also stall your forward progress and possibly draw the focus from the real objections down the road.

You do not want to take action on an objection that is not real or overemphasize one that is of little importance. To help determine the relevance of each, your first reaction should be to let it sit, paying no attention to it. Just move forward. However, as you proceed, covertly try to examine the context and manner in which the customer's objection was stated to help determine its validity. Look at their facial expression and mannerisms to determine the level of seriousness of each. Measure their anxiety before you seek to act. If it's a valid concern, they will show signs of their concern or repeat it again. If they show limited

108

signs or do not repeat it, move on and proceed with the process, their objection had no importance.

HANDLING A TRUE OBJECTION

Okay, objections are going to occur, we know that. Therefore, we should prepare for them. The best way to do this is to build a relationship with your customers that will allow you the persuasiveness to overcome them. Prepare by having good product knowledge and good people skills. With the combination of these forces, your ability to search for and develop the information to answer their concerns and then influence them to rethink their present position will be greatly enhanced. You need to prepare yourself in this manner because each objection will be unique. There is no set answer to an objection. It is up to you to develop creativity and adapt your problem solving skills to overcome each one.

PROVIDE NEW INFORMATION

Many inexperienced salespeople will push for a decision while still using the same established facts. A top salesperson, however, will seek to determine what is missing with a series of investigative questions and then offer his or her customer a solution. Do not push for a decision based solely on the information your customers currently have. Seek out their concerns, supply new information, and then ask for a new decision based on the new information.

CREDIBILITY

Your ability to overcome an objection is directly related to the credibility you have created. What you say must be accepted and believed by your customers before you can influence them to rethink their position. This is why it's so important to start building your credibility early on with your concern for their needs, assessment questions, and accurate information. You have to build a level of trust and expertise before they'll allow you to influence their decision. Understand that you'll have to be able to understand, analyze, and present your case with each hesitation you encounter and have receptive customers who will listen to the new information that you provide.

THE OBJECTION PROCESS

Just as there is a step-by-step program for the sales process, there is also one for handling the objections that occur. When your customers present an obstacle, real or not, that has slowed or diverted their direction, and your initial attempt to let it sit was unsuccessful, you must look to overcome it.

The first step is to fully understand the objection. Let the customer completely finish stating their concern. Do not interject your opinion before you know where they are going. Learn the complete objection so you can better analyze it for its purpose and validity. Next, clarify the objection. When your customers state an objection, restate it to them. Clarify what they are saying. Some examples may be, "How do you mean?" or "What exactly are you saying?" Your customers may actually answer their own objection. Even if not, this will certainly give you more information on how to proceed. Next, answer their objection with the appropriate action or response and verify that you have answered it. Once you've confirmed that you have answered it, move on quickly. Change the subject and proceed. Do not let them linger with the objection still in their mind. A great way to do this is to promptly ask an unrelated question. This will clear their mind and persuade them to focus on your new question. They will be involved in a new conversation.

1. Let them finish stating their concern.

2. Clarify what it is they are saying.

110

3. Confirm that is a true objection.

4. Question for its true purpose.

5. Answer the objection.

6. Confirm that you have answered it.

7. Move forward.

With each step of the process comes a new stage to complete and new variables to overcome. Although each step may be different, the process involved in having customers agree to proceed should always remain a constant.

PERSISTENCE

In trying to solve each objection, be persistent. Too many salespeople lack persistence because they take what their customers tell them at face value. Well, sometimes a customer's motives are disguised, hidden, or misrepresented. You need to have the persistence and tenacity to uncover these difficult objections before you can proceed. Remember when you were a kid and saw your favorite candy bar in the checkout lane? There was no objection that was going to stand between you and that candy. There was no objection you couldn't handle. Reach back for that same level of persistence.

PART TWO

THE THREE MOST COMMON OBJECTIONS

In the business of sales, there are a few specific objections that we will hear over and over. Our business will generally produce some of the same objections no matter what or where you sell. The ones you will hear most often are: "I want to think about it.", "The price is too high," and, "I want to check with other dealers." Get comfortable with them because you will soon face them. Make a list of common variations and practice answering them. Lets take a look.

I WANT TO THINK ABOUT IT

This objection is typically due to a concern where your customers will not be forthcoming with their reasoning. When your customer states, "I want to think about it," there is most likely a specific reason holding them up. However, they have chosen not to disclose it to you. Something has occurred or exists that is stopping them from buying. For some reason, they opted to state a more obscure and harder-to-overcome objection. It is here that you must become investigative.

DETERMINE THE TRUE CONCERN

The key in overcoming this objection is first to verify that there really is a concern. Then determine where the true concern lies. Search for and find the real objection. You must uncover and satisfy your customer's underlying concerns before you can move beyond this objection. An attempt to find a valid reason should always be made first, and that is what we will do here.

If their objection is a real concern, it could literally be anything. It may be the color of the car's interior, the value for their trade, the date of delivery, the coffee machine was out of sugar, or they are waiting for another dealer to call them back. It is here that you must clarify and investigate to uncover what is actually impeding them. You need to have the perception to realize that there really is an underlying concern, then you have to have the investigative qualities and persistence to uncover it.

What makes this particular objection even more difficult is that you not only have to determine their reasoning, you also have to get them to admit it. This, of course, is while they do not want to lose their

112

own credibility and admit that there really is an underlying reason. Remember, they are saying that there is no reason. They just want to think about it. However, the odds are great that there is a reason, and you must find it before you can proceed and sell them a vehicle. I know this might be a little confusing or even farfetched for the beginning salesperson to understand, but it's an everyday reality in the closing process. Take the time to work this out for yourself and try to rationalize it. When you understand this, you will soon unlock the many sales you are missing.

Start and finish your discovery process with a series of questions. Search for their reasons with one question after another until you uncover it.

Ask what they will be thinking about. Look inquisitive. Ask why they wouldn't move forward. Ask why they would. Ask if there is any other reason they may have other than just wanting to think on it.

Try to get them to agree on certain aspects of the deal and seek what is not yet agreeable by process of elimination. Imply that they really should let you know because you will eventually figure it out anyway.

If they are still not receptive or forthcoming, be upfront and candid, "Mr. Customer, I have found that, many times, when a customer wants to think about it, there is usually some underlying reason. Is that the case here? Honestly, what's bothering you? Is it the color, the deal, the options? What is it? Is it the trade? Is it your down payment? Is it the wrong time of day?"

Pause here. Stay silent. Will them to answer with your helpful, curious, silent face. Look confused. Continue with, "Is it me? Did I do something wrong? Is it there something I haven't explained?" This method will usually work. Give it a try. If it does not, do not give in. Be strong and persistent. It will eventually come to light. Just make sure to monitor your customer's anxiety so you can best judge when to turn up or turn down the heat. Keep them willing participants with your rapport and humor. Show that you care and are concerned. Let them know that you want to help them, and the best way for you to start is for them to help you determine the origin of their concern. Look concerned. Look disappointed. Look confused. Continue to ask about specific possibilities as you replay the last stages of the process in your mind.

If you still have no luck, try this approach, "Sir, let me ask you a question. I understand that you are not making a decision today and that you want to think about it, but if you were to make a decision today, what one parameter of this deal would you change?" Then pause again. Stay silent. Silence will usually lead him to answer. This question is easy for your customers to answer because the first part takes the pressure off.

Note that this is not a timed effort. This investigation is not over until you have uncovered their true reasoning. If you need to or the situation warrants it, take an occasional break back to your common ground and then try some more. However, know the only way you can overcome this objection is to find out what the true objection is, and for this you will need to continue.

While in your search, try to recall and then tie any less-than-positive reactions to the variable you were discussing at the time. Think back, was it the options on their selection, the trade, the value determined for one of them, or was it the down payment? There is no set answer here. You just have to keep searching until something shows up.

If they need to sleep on it, let them know that's okay, your pillow is in your car. Continue with your wit, charm, and creativity and they will hopefully fill you in. By now, you really have to have some rapport built up to keep going. So from early on, make them like you. Tell them you like them and want to be their salesperson. Have fun with them. Make them laugh. But remember, wanting to think on it is rarely a valid objection.

Ok. Now. If all fails in your attempts to find an underlying reason for this objection, there might be another explanation. In other, less likely cases, your customers may not have an understandable reason. They may just have a hard time making a decision. It may be that your customers are not good at decisions and there is no set reason stopping them. However unlikely, this is a possibility. I was hesitant to include this as an explanation because I don't want you to think this must be common and give you an excuse to give up too early in your investigation for a real motive. However, because this explanation is a reality in some cases, I will discuss it further at the end of the chapter. But first, let's look at our second most common objection.

THE PRICE IS TOO HIGH

Many times, when a customer states that the price is too high, know it just comes from their instinct. It is just a natural reaction. For typical customers, this is simply the easiest response for them to accomplish their actual motive, which is typically to either leave or start positioning for a discount.

By stating that the price is too high, your customer's reasoning is usually well defined. They may be saying they can get it cheaper, they can't afford it, or they are just not sold enough on the value of the vehicle to purchase it.

If they can get it cheaper, ask how much cheaper. If they say they can't afford it, help them with their budget to verify. If they really can't afford it, switch vehicles. Seek to adjust as necessary. These are acceptable questions, and they will usually give you an answer. If they're just taking a shot at a discount, and most of the time this is the case, just work your deal.

ESTABLISH THEIR MOTIVE

The key to this objection is to establish their intentions and motives. The key in overcoming this objection, as with most similar objections, is to question it until they come forward with their specific concern or motive. Understand if they've made it all the way through the sales process and all of their other goals are lining up, their motive is typically price. They usually just want a discount.

If they do want a discount, remember, this does not necessarily mean they will not buy without one. In many cases, they may not know what a good price really is, and this might just be their attempt to find out by reading your reaction. They might have thought they should ask, however, they may lack the resolve or real desire to make it a condition of the sale. Understand there is often a risk in discounting your vehicle too fast. Your customers might become concerned with why you have chosen to discount the price and start to question whether there is some unforeseen reason. Makes sense, right? This is why you must always follow the process of the sale. It is here, their stated objection is really just a request to negotiate. If this is the case, simply continue as explained in closing the sale.

I WANT TO CHECK WITH OTHER DEALERS

This is the one of the toughest objections to work against, because in most cases, this is what they really have in mind. The advice to shop around is the most common advice given to anyone looking for an automobile. Some people will keep this as their guide.

APPEAL TO THE CUSTOMER'S SENSE OF REASON

The best approach here is to appeal to their sense of reason and fairness. Let them know that all dealers pay the same, so their deal here could be as good as anywhere. Even for a pre-owned car, the wholesale value is typically somewhat stable. Establish that your deal is a fair one and proceed to persuade them it is. Let them know you have given them a great deal. Let them know you will be there for them after the sale. Always include the value in yourself as a salesperson. Let them know that their goal should be a great deal up front and great service afterward.

If your emotional responses are not being well received, try to reason with them logically. Let them know that if they went to a hundred dealers, they still might not get the absolute lowest price, because one of the thousand other dealers will likely beat one of their deals. Let them know that their goal should simply be to get a good deal, because the possibility of the best deal doesn't really exist. This is because the parameters of any deal are subject to change as time goes by, and lots of time will go by as they check with all of these other dealers. If their goal is to save money, ask if their time is worth nothing. Let them know they can and should be happy with the great deal you've given them and that you will take care of them after they buy. Remind them of the value you have already given them with your knowledge and effort. Remind them of the value of your service department and staff.

If you're still not getting through, you may have to verify that shopping around is really their intention. Although it is not typical here, this may still be the case. Here again, you will have to investigate. Use all of the exploratory methods discussed in the previous objections, because you must always uncover their true objections before you can overcome them. If not much is working, try asking them if all parameters of the deal were equal, including price, where would they rather buy? Now ask them why. Separate that fact and build the value in it.

In all circumstances, be thorough and persistent, because if they leave, they probably won't be back. Someone else will be selling these customers a car. This is especially true if you have given them too much information. You can bet that your price will never stand as the lowest. Your information will just become leverage for their negotiation elsewhere. For this particular objection, you will often have to be diverse in your approach. Try to persuade them logically and emotionally, and follow up with what appears to work best.

If all fails and you are unable to persuade them, at least leave them with some curiosity. Give them the idea that a better deal may come out. However, save the details until they come back. If you are unable to persuade them, your only hope is their curiosity. If you can develop a strong enough curiosity, they might possibly come back. Follow up with these customers promptly.

Note that this often is an objection you may avoid by giving a great presentation, bringing your rapport to a high level, and building the value of purchasing from you and your dealership. The real overcoming of this objection starts when you say hello.

WHERE IS THE OBJECTION?

The hardest objection to overcome is when there really isn't one. What I mean by this is that there may not be a tangible reason that is stopping your customer from making a decision. As we stated earlier, this may be a reason for your customer stating, "I want to think about it."

Having no real objection is probably hard for most people to understand. This is because many people think there is a standard in buying. Many will believe that the level of indecisiveness someone can have will stop at the level that they themselves have. At some point, they believe that their customers will either want it or they won't. However, for many people, this isn't the case. For many people, it is just hard to make a decision.

Think about how many will go through the whole process and still say they want to think about it. Even after multiple attempts to search for the reason behind their not buying, they still leave. Well, how many more vehicles a month would you sell if you sold to everybody who wanted to think about it? Is it safe to guess it's probably a lot?

In order to do this, you must first open your understanding. You must become aware that there isn't always a real reason. Certain people are just uncomfortable in making a decision, any decision. Maybe it was a bad purchase in the past or maybe they were raised to not spend money. Maybe they're just victims of their own eccentricities or rituals. These reasons may make no sense to you. However, to excel, you must become aware of them. Open your mind and accept that people's thoughts or actions do not always make sense.

Since these particular customers are uncomfortable with making decisions, your logical response should be to help make them comfortable. The key to selling these customers is to understand their decision process and enable them to feel comfortable. Have empathy for these customers. If you open up and share a story about when you had a hard time making a decision, they might lose some of their anxiety. They may find common ground with you.

Usually these customers want to make a decision. However, they want or need to be persuaded. Have patience. They want to know they're making the right decision and they want to feel comfortable about the decision. Seek to confirm that the offered terms are agreeable and their selection fits their needs. For the fearful customer, let them know that their fears are unfounded. For the pattern driven or ritualistic customer, let them know that their actions do not make sense; they are not logical. These customers typically recognize their internal halting or persuasion factors don't make sense, they just need help in overcoming them. Actually, in many cases, they really wish they could overcome them and proceed with the sale.

Rushing these people will not help. Patiently helping them to visualize, work out, and come to terms with their possibilities will.

Too many salespeople give up here because they will only use their own buying steps as a comparison. To be successful, you cannot. Your customers at this point may be having their own internal battle. They may be literally going back and forth in their own mind on what to do. It's sometimes difficult for people to make a decision, no matter what the decision is, so work with them. Understand them. Examine what they are saying. Learn to recognize the minor ploys that customers may fabricate to put off a decision, and understand them. Know that their self-limiting ploys are often just internal mechanisms and are not based on tangible information.

In some cases, they may just want to avoid reliving any anguish that may have been caused by a previous decision. They may want to avoid making a mistake. However, because this fear is generally nonspecific, they usually can't logically tie this decision to a specific feeling in the past. This is good, because with the proper show of concern and the proper assurance, you can persuade these customers. You can complete your job.

Please know that at this late stage in the process, these customers really want to buy. Their pause or indecision in no way means they do not want to buy their selected vehicle. It also does not mean they don't want to buy it now. In fact, it's usually safe to assume that if they went through the whole process and made it to this point they really want to buy a car. They just want and need some help. They want someone to make them feel comfortable and confident first, but they want to buy. So allow them all the comfort and opportunity you can.

Have you ever gone into an electronics store, a home-tool store, or wherever and come home empty-handed? Did you walk in hoping you were going to come home with that big-screen TV or digital camera, and yet came up with some excuse not to leave with it? You put it off for some reason. You wanted it, but somehow couldn't justify it. Well, while thinking of a time you did not act on a purchase, place yourself in the position of being your own salesperson. Now, as the salesperson, picture yourself as someone who always makes the sale. Your listening, understanding, and problem-solving skills are so good that you have the best qualities of the top five salespeople in your dealership. Well, guess what? You made the sale. Congratulations. How did you do it? How did you convince yourself? Seriously, how? Take the time to think this out and then take hold of your process and save it. Use it the next time you get a challenging customer who really wants to buy.

Please understand that, when someone leaves, they will often move on, at least in the short term, because there are too many other distractions in life. In some cases they may decide to make a similar purchase, however, it probably resulted from a trip to another place of business or a conversation with another salesperson. The moral of this story is that you have to take action when the opportunity exists. You have to take a current interest and develop it into a "today" buying decision.

FINAL THOUGHT

Let me share one fact with you. People do not come into your dealership to get their clothes dry cleaned. They do not come in for a loaf of bread or some milk. Most people do not even like to come into a dealership. They are there for a reason. They are there for a vehicle. They will, at some time, buy one, and they want to now. To be successful, you have to recognize, understand, and be able to overcome your customer's objections. You need to have the understanding, the patience, and the ability to make your customers feel comfortable with you, your dealership, and the terms of the deal. It is your job to help them and believe in them. If they have come this far in the sales process, you have to believe they want to be helped. Give all your customers all of the opportunity in the world to own and enjoy their new vehicle. Give them the status, the style, the comfort, the protection, the reliability, and the solution they want. Do not let reactionary defensive actions or solvable objections stand in the way. Seek out their concerns and hesitations and answer them.

So, have you? Have you ever wished you bought something but didn't and regretted it later? Well, maybe all you needed was a good salesperson to help you make the move. Become that salesperson.

11

STILL CLOSING

The reason that many people do not close is because they cannot let go of their recent demands. A person will not be open to a new idea, while they are still thinking of their previous one. However, this is exactly what must happen before you and they can move forward.

Closing certain customers will often take more than one attempt. In fact, a close may take many attempts through many different approaches; different approaches that will afford new opportunities to raise their offer or lower their demands when negotiating, different approaches that may also establish what is hindering them from moving forward.

When closing a resilient customer, you want to plan your approach and convey your offering in a way that will best allow them to enhance or alter their previous way of thinking. This is best accomplished by a new approach in which you may have to selectively lose some of your memory. What I mean is that you should always make an effort to start every new closing attempt with a clean slate. Every time you are able to rebuild or add value or offer new information, ask them to move forward again, showing no memory of their previous demands or the reasons for their hesitation.

You want to clear your memory, attempt to clear theirs, and then offer a new opportunity to make a new decision. You do not want to be influenced and do not want to influence them by allowing their previous offer or demands to be present in any form. Conditioning yourself to believe and enact this line of thinking is very important if you want to be a good closer. You have to believe in this to be consistently successful.

To complete your task of providing a new direction, you will have to disregard your customer's previous demands and then supply

123

sufficient new information as a reason for them to alter their position. You have to allow them to distance their past thoughts from their future thoughts. You need to create a gap in their train of thought. Take them to a different topic before you reattempt your approach. Leave your closing attempts aside for a moment and go back into your rapport-building stage.

Ok, let's now look at this supplemental closing attempt as a process.

The best plan of attack for when a customer's requests are unacceptable is to:

State that their wants are unacceptable.	Decline
Let them know why.	Enlighten
Bring the conversation back to a personal level.	Erase
Rebuild value or supply new information.	Re-setup
Ask for a new decision.	Re-attempt

This is a process that you can, and may have to, repeat many times before your customer's reasons for not moving forward are resolved. Persistence.

In many cases, when the negotiation stalls, you will want to bring in your manager or a skilled closer; however, if one is not available, it is up to you to reset your scene and close the terms of the deal yourself. Again, the key here is to absolutely erase your memory or history with your customers and pretend you are meeting them for the first time, as your manager or closer would be. It is usually better to separate yourself before each new attempt and after you have reset the scene. Just get yourself some water or something. When you come back, come as a new person. Start with a new demeanor. Come back with a straight business face. Let your customer know with both your verbal and physical presence that you are there for one reason and one reason only; to close the deal. Remember that at this stage, we have completely gone through the whole process, and our only goal is to get them to agree to the final figures.

The script that you are about to read is your best approach when reattempting a close, so learn it and follow it every time. This script is question-based and will engage your customers. This script allows you to take and keep control and lead them, step-by-step, to the sale. It does not matter that they've already answered all of these questions in the past. This whole process can and should be repeated until they close. Let's look at the script.

If you are an assigned closer, it might start like this:

"Hi, how are you? My name is JB, and I just wanted to take the time to meet you and see if we can put this deal together." Pause. "Is that okay with you? Great."

Or, if you're making another attempt to finish, it might go like this:

"Okay, I'm back. What I would like to do, if it's okay with you, is go ahead and attempt to work this deal out right now. Is that okay? Okay, great. I'd like to take a second to reconfirm a couple of facts and then get into the details of how we can best accomplish this. Is that okay with you? Great."

Note: Reconfirming that this is, "okay," will start the momentum of their yes-saying groove. Trust this. Restart here with a pause, then go.

"Let me ask you a question." Note: Pause here to get their attention. Second note: Remember, even if you at previous times have asked these same questions, repeat them now in this sequence. "If we were able to work out a deal on the vehicle that you've selected and it's acceptable to you, would you be in a position to move forward? Okay, great. Is there anyone else involved in this decision other than yourself? Okay, great. Are there any other questions that you have about this vehicle? Okay, great. So what you're saying is that if you wanted to, and if the terms were acceptable to you, you could take this vehicle home today. Is that correct? Okay, great. If you were to purchase this vehicle, would you be paying cash or financing? Okay, great. And that cash is available, or your credit is in good standing and you could receive the credit needed to complete this transaction? Okay, great. So what you're saying is that there's nothing stopping you from making this deal if you wanted to, right? Okay, great." Slightly nod your head up and down to help encourage a positive response to each of your questions. This questioning process, at this stage, is very businesslike and fast-paced. It is meant to start the groundwork for your reconfirming agreement.

It is now time to confirm or reconfirm what you already know is acceptable to your customer. This may be either the terms of the deal or the established benefits of the vehicle's features that have satisfied their wants or needs. Continue to ask these re-confirming questions until you feel them start to take ownership. These questions will often lead them to realize that they in fact want to, are able to, and emotionally and logically should take ownership, "You like the color of the vehicle, right? You like the options of the vehicle, don't you? You are okay with the location of the dealership, correct? You feel comfortable with our service so far, don't you? You are agreeable to the down payment, correct? You can afford it if you choose to, right?"

Note that with your encouragement, your customers have answered in the affirmative in a steady and repetitious manner. You have now set yourself up again to re-close. They have essentially taken ownership by now, so now is the time to re-attempt your close. If this questioning turns up a non-positive answer that is the objection that remains. Upon answering it, simply back up a couple questions to get the flow started again and then continue.

"Okay then, let's go ahead, and agree to our offering. Let me have a copy of your driver's license, and I promise not to delay you any further."

Pause here and look intently with your hand out, gesturing for their acceptance. Do not speak. Once you have set up your close with this path, your final close can be the one above or any other one question close. What you're doing here is tying up all the loose ends in their mind and escalating the flow of their approval. Note that this will paint a picture of a number of reasons why they should take the vehicle. If again they do not close, try repeating the whole process again, but this time in a slower mode. Look bewildered after every one of their positive responses. Portray to them that their final answer just isn't making sense.

126

Again, look confused. Portray that you want to help them with their decision but need help in understanding their hesitation. Now reattempt the close again. Remember, if they are still there, they are there for a reason.

IS IT STILL PRICE?

In many cases, the sale price of the vehicle will still be stated as the reason for not moving forward. If this is the case, reattempt your payment approach. For people who are financing, let them know that what really matters is their monthly payment.

If you are unable to close them on your requested sale price, ask them what their preferred payment range would be. If they give you a payment range, ask if you could somehow juggle the figures to get to their payment range, would they purchase the vehicle. If they say okay, you are done. Even though this was brought up to your customers earlier, it may be more readily accepted at this stage. Write the deal up at list or your last requested price and send them to finance. Remember; always vary your actions to fit the situation. If they are not closing on price, switch to payments. If they're not closing on payments, switch to price.

ONE LAST CLOSE

Here is one last close for when your customer is almost, but not quite there. This is a close I will generally save until all other attempts have failed. This close is also good if they start to back up in finance, and even works in the parking lot if needed. Most of the time, I will try to deliver it as one of their friends would, kind of like when a person might poke fun at a friend's lack of action when they both know it's obviously best to take action. Here it is:

"Okay, look. The people around us might not know it, and you might not be acting like it, but you want to buy this car. You can fool them, but you can't fool me. I've been doing this for a while, and I can feel it. I know you didn't get in your car, drive across town, spend two hours with someone you don't know, give out all your personal information, and go through all these steps and not want to own this car. You did not come for a loaf of bread, we don't sell milk, and you said yourself that you don't even like car shopping. So let's get it on. It wasn't me who dragged you out of bed," while smiling, "so let's get going. All I need is your agreement, and I will take care of everything else."

Okay, by now, I will assume that your customers are enjoying their new car. Congratulations.

12

LET ME ASK YOU A QUESTION

"Let me ask you a question?" This is the most powerful question in sales. It is also my favorite. It will stop your customer, get their attention, and allow you to steer them in the direction you want with the questions you ask. It will give you the opportunity to lead them with their own answers.

Being successful in sales requires you to act and react constantly in the best way to sell. You have to be more than just knowledgeable and helpful. You have to determine the best way to proceed and chart your course. Understand that very few people will come in and walk you through the steps to sell them a car; very few. To be successful in sales, you have to investigate, learn, and establish a direction. You have to be creative, anticipatory, and uninhibited in your quest to understand your customers and their needs.

Asking the appropriate questions is the basis of sales for every step of the process. Think about it. You question to build rapport, gain credibility, determine the benefits they seek, root out their objections, and confirm their selection to influence a purchase. Your success is directly related to your ability to use their answers to confirm each step and advance to the next. By asking the proper questions, we are able to control the pace and direction of the sale, all while receiving the information we need to best understand our customer's goals.

A question is also the easiest way to initiate a conversation. It invites interaction and shows that you care about your customer's needs. In sales, there are many types of questions we will use. The use and timing of each will depend on where we are in the sales process and what we want our customer's responses to be. With some questions, we want to learn our customer's answers, with others we want them to realize their answers. In the first example, we would use a discovery or exploratory question; in the second, we would use a leading or confirming question. These are the two most important questions in sales. Let's take a look.

DISCOVERY QUESTIONS

A discovery question is used to gain information. It is how we are best able to determine the objectives our customers may have and create a positive interaction with each. It gives us the information we need to determine how best to move forward all while maintaining the flow of our conversation.

With discovery questions, we also build our level of credibility. This line of questioning in itself allows us to show that we are capable of understanding their needs and thus capable of helping them with their selections. Understand that your advice will have no credence if your customers feel that you do not have the information needed to give them the guidance they desire.

In addition to better understanding their goals, discovery questions can also be helpful in understanding the buying style of your customers in the early stages and investigating their hesitancies in the later stages. Your discovery questions are essential in helping you navigate every step of the process, from start to finish. When in doubt, ask. Do not inhibit your success by allowing yourself to navigate in the dark. Explore your curiosities and discover your answers.

LEADING QUESTIONS

A leading question is one that is used to help direct our customers to a certain path. The use of this question is for when we seek to have our customers form an opinion or move to a decision based upon their own answers. It is to help guide them, or at least have them reconsider a current point of view.

The key in effectively accomplishing our goal here is to calculate what we want our customer's answers to be, then carefully construct the questions that will help guide them to responses or thoughts we desire. After we understand their goals and determine their next best step, we want to be able to effectively influence their next step.. If you're successful in accomplishing this, the result is simple. They will always be more receptive to their own discovery than any statement you may offer. Basically, if you say it, they will listen; if they say it, they will believe.

An example while selecting may be, "This is the color and option package you were looking for, isn't it?" Or an example for when preparing to negotiate may be: "If we were able to agree upon the terms of this deal, you would be in a position to move forward today, wouldn't you?" Note that you are leading your customers to confirm their commitment; the commitment needed in order to proceed.

There will also be the times when we will have to prepare for our future. We will sometimes want to influence our customer's future outlook to better prepare for their possibilities. An example of this can be found when narrowing our customer's choice in a vehicle. It is here that you will want to create a question or series of questions in advance of their decision to help encourage a new way of thinking.

"Sir i understand you weren't looking for captains chairs or DVD in your new SUV, but do you think your kids might appreciate them?" "Do you think your trips up north each spring might be a little more peaceful?"

Understand in many cases, having your customers answer their own questions may be the only way to conclusively gain their agreement. A customer will often doubt the validity of what their salesperson says because they will be cautious of their motives. They'll always be curious as to whose best interest you have in mind. The leading question, however, will allow you to answer your customer's concerns, both before and after they are realized. All average salespeople will continually seek to answer their customer's concerns with their answers. All successful salespeople know the best way to ensure their customer's conclusive agreement is to invite them to come up with the answers on their own. I mean, who doesn't like peaceful trips?

WHY A QUESTION?

With a question we are not assuming what may be important to our customers; we are seeking to understand the beliefs that are important to them. I often visit sales related businesses and it really surprises me how very few salespeople will seek to understand or evaluate a customer's needs before they start to show or explain their various products. This is the biggest and most common mistake of all beginning salespeople. This is why most beginning salespeople fail to succeed and why average salespeople fail to excel.

A top salesperson recognizes that customers want to be understood. They want a salesperson that will help guide them with the proper advice on their specific needs, not one who will just assume what they want or need. They want a salesperson who is not afraid to ask, understands how to ask, and is capable of giving credible advice and guidance to the responses they receive.

QUESTION QUESTION QUESTION

Make no mistake, sales is the creative ability of asking the proper questions. It is absolutely essential in succeeding. If you could only come away with learning one skill from reading this book, understanding why we question would probably be your best choice. It is that important.

Here is a more in-depth look at the reasons we question. Read through each reason slowly, visualizing a scenario for each. The easiest way to get better at asking questions and understanding their importance is simple. Become inquisitive and ask.

- You question to seek the information needed to gain common ground and build rapport.

- You question to allow customers to open up and show their interactive style.

- You question to show customers you care and want to understand.

- You question to discover the benefits customers are looking for.

- You question to build the credibility needed to influence.

- You question to narrow the scope of selection to one vehicle.

- You question to get customers to allow themselves to reevaluate a current opinion on an idea or preconceived notion.

- You question to build desire.

- You question to build the value in their choice of vehicle.

- You question to confirm selection during the presentation.

- You question to involve them in visualizing ownership.

- You question to revalue their trade.

- You question to build value in their choice of you and your dealership.

- You question to see if your customers are ready to buy.

- You question to build value in the financial terms offered.

- You question to seek out their objections in moving forward.

- You question to re-clarify the reasons for their choice and ask for the sale.

I hope you are thinking that we use questions a lot, because we do. The sale is likely dependent upon it. With a question, you maintain the flow and keep the direction of the sale. It is how you engage your customers through each step of the process and continue to the next. The top salesperson has come to realize that selling a car is like solving a problem, and the easiest way to solve a problem is to seek out and analyze the facts. While in the process of the sale, learn the direction of your path. Think of yourself as a sales detective. Do not let fear or hesitancy limit your ability to learn and succeed. It is your job to help your customers discover and realize their solutions.

HOW TO QUESTION

The best way to begin with any questioning plan is to start with the small, easy questions first. Your customers want you to understand their needs and look forward to your questions; however, they also want to feel comfortable with you. Build some rapport and seek to engage them in a regular conversation. Understand that if you listen and show an interest in their light initial responses, you'll be more likely to have willing and open responses in the future. If you are able to establish an early level of comfort, you will be better able to lead them with your questions later in the process.

The best way to have your customers open up is to involve them with your genuine concern and adaptive approach. If your customer's answers are closed and narrow in the beginning, use a wider, more open approach. When listening, take the time to hear their response and understand their thoughts. Do not just listen as an acknowledgment, as this is way too transparent to the average customer. Also, do not just rattle off all your questions at once. Your customers may become defensive if they feel they are being interrogated. To help get started, use some of the examples of why we question listed here as a reference and build upon them.

CATER YOUR APPROACH

Sometimes, in special cases, you will need to take extra care in your approach. This is advice for the "don't pressure me" customer, as here you will have to walk with a little more thought.

One way to soften an objection to a question is to introduce a way out. It might go something like this: "Would it be possible to bring your trade in today, or would you prefer not to?" Or, when making a call you might open with, "Hello, Mr. Customer, this is JB. Did I catch you at a bad time?"

This style of questioning is not to change your goal. It is merely a creative way to achieve it. By having an option to not interact, certain customers will likely feel less pressured and be more inclined to respond. This practice can also be used for the person who always feels he has to be in control or the reverse type thinker. "Sir is it okay if I show you one more feature, or are you not interested?" Note that this will both allow for and encourage a look.

The key to successful questioning with any customer is to adjust your approach as you proceed. How best to question will always be determined by the circumstance of your customers and the stage in which you are involved. Within your conversation, you want there to be balance. A balance of asking, listening, and speaking, all while keeping your conversation flowing at the proper pace and in the proper direction. Always seek to keep a harmony between you and your customers and then proceed with your questions as appropriate.

QUESTION TYPES AND HINTS

Unfortunately, our business is a business that still has some preconceived notions in its representation. It is not hard to picture a pushy salesperson rattling off all the benefits they think will appeal to their customer. This image alone is half the reason many customers come in with preset time limits and other escape plans.

A top salesperson, however, has come to understand that the way to create a receptive audience is to engage them, and the easiest way to do this is with a question. Questions will keep you informed and on track, all while keeping the proper focus within your interaction by encouraging you to listen as much as you speak. Where a statement will need a a receptive audience, a question will in fact encourage one. Here are some additional helpful questions and their uses.

OPEN-ENDED QUESTION

The open ended question is one that will get your customers talking. It has no specific answer and will offer them the opportunity to answer any way they want. It is a great question to use in the rapport stage to help your customers open up. It will invite your customers to tell you a story. It can also help you learn the preferred style and personality of your customers. It will allow them to offer their outlook or experiences and give them the latitude to describe them in the manner they choose. An example may be: "So, how do you like living out there in the country?"

CLOSED-ENDED QUESTION

This question will give you a specific answer. It will direct your customer to a defined response. The question can often be answered with a yes or a no. It is also used to help focus on a smaller set of options.

Both open and closed-ended questions can be used in the discovery stage or when leading customers to a certain response. Your goal should be to start with open questions to get the overall idea and then move to a more closed set of questions to focus on your specific objective. Some examples of the closed question may be: "Will you be trading in your current vehicle?" or "Is this an option package that you would consider?"

136

CLARIFYING QUESTION

The clarifying question is used to help further understand your customer's thoughts, concerns or objectives. It allows you to show that you care about what your customers have to offer and will allow them to explain or clear up what they are saying. It allows you and your customers to be in complete understanding while searching for and finding a solution. It'll also uncover if something has changed and you need to establish a new direction.

MULTIPLE-CHOICE QUESTION

This is where you would ask a question and provide two possible answers. It is a question that you would use to narrow down the available choices for your customers, making it easier for them to answer. Remember the multiple choice questions you had back in school? Weren't they easier than the essay questions? It takes a lot less thought to choose an answer than to create one, therefore, this question is more likely to get a response.

Additionally, this question can be used to lead them to a set of options preferred by you. For example, asking, "Sir, would it be easier for you to come in on Wednesday or Thursday?" or "Mrs. Customer, would you prefer the sport model with the sunroof or without?" will more likely produce a definitive response, and one in which either answer was pre-determined as acceptable by you. With this one question, you can steer them in the direction you want, make it easy for them to answer, and get a commitment from them all at the same time.

INVOLVEMENT QUESTION

This is where you will place your customers in an ownership position. It is to help paint a picture of the experiences they will have while enjoying their new vehicle. To best accomplish this, simply ask a question that creates an image they can visualize. "So, what's the first movie you think your grandson will watch on your new vehicle's entertainment center?" or "Where is the first vacation you will take with your new van?" or even, "Wow, what do you think this will look like in the driveway?"

Your customers will respond to these on an emotional level. Try to visualize the picture each of these will create and how this may encourage their decision. Remember, very few people buy strictly for transportation reasons. Buying decisions are often motivated by the wants and desires that their selection will fulfill. Help them envision their dreams. Paint them a picture.

CONFIRMING QUESTION

The confirming question is the complement to the leading question. It's used to confirm or reconfirm your customer's responses or choices while setting up a close or smaller confirmation. It is how you get the flow of yeses leading to the big yes down the road. This is where you add a confirming set of words to help lead your customers directly to the response you want.

During a difficult close, in which your customer is indecisive about moving forward, try asking a small series of these before you again ask for the sale. The momentum you create will greatly increase the odds of your customer saying yes.

As your customer weighs his decision, you might start off with: "Sir, let me ask you a question." Pause, "You did say blue was your color of choice, correct?" or "Your neighbors have had a reliable experience with theirs, haven't they?"

Then add questions like:

"The investment required falls within the budget you set for yourself, doesn't it?"

"The four-wheel drive option will allow you to take your trips up north this winter, right?"

138

"With the current incentives, now is the best time to buy, don't you agree?"

This line of questioning can be used while setting up for the final close or be adjusted for each agreement needed to help you move through the steps. Please recognize the importance of creating a positive momentum. The use of the confirming question will greatly increase your ability to lead your customer to the sale, wouldn't you agree?

RETURN THE QUESTION

This next type of question is similar to the confirming question, but is meant to work off your customer's questions. Its goal is to further confirm your customer's wants by using the opportunities they give. Basically, it's answering your customer's question with a question of your own, with the goal of leading them to a desired response.

If your customer were to ask, "Do you have an Explorer like this with chrome step bars?" You could return, "Would you like one with chrome step bars?" Or if they were to ask, "Would you be able to have this vehicle inspected by this afternoon?" You could return, "Would you like to have it ready this afternoon?"

Notice the difference. If you just answered yes, you may not have anything. However, if you returned their question with a question of your own, a positive response will give you the commitment needed to keep them moving forward. It solicits and confirms their interest.

The use of this question can also complete the sale as well. For example, in regard to the exchange above, a good follow up may be "Sir, if I had one with chrome step bars and could have it ready by this afternoon, did you want to get started on some of the paperwork?"

HOW MUCH?

When your customers ask how much, should we return their question with a question of our own as well? Well, let's take a look.

Take note that customers often do not initially come in to buy that exact day. They come in to get information that they'll keep adding to until they happen across a salesperson skillful in gaining a commitment in the course of exchanging information. Understanding this, we need to alter their time frame to one more in the present. One certain way to slow your customers down and start gaining a commitment is by returning this question with a question of your own.

If they ask, "How much is that blue Camry?" try
"Is that the Camry you like?"
"Is blue your color of choice?"
"Have you settled on the Camry?"
"Are you interested in a cash price or a monthly payment?"
"Hey, I like the Camry, too. What is it about that Camry that you like?"

This form of questioning is not being vague. It allows you to build their interest before assigning a price. Notice how you can create almost any response you want depending on how you vary your questions. This is important for adapting to where in the process you are. It gives you the opportunity to have an open response for the earlier stages and a more focused response for the later stages. If you just give out a price, you again may have nothing. Use their desire for pricing as a way to gain their attention and start to build their sense of value and commitment.

IF I COULD

Have you ever had or heard of the customer who never got enough? They just kept asking to have something else thrown in, eternally postponing the sale. "Will you throw in the mats? Will you throw in the tint? Will you throw in the hitch? How about the hitch cover?" And so on.

Well, I ask you, wouldn't the salesperson have saved some profit, time, and maybe even the sale by simply asking, "Sir, if I could throw in the mats, would you buy the truck?"

If I could, would you? Although this question may be considered too forward by some, I disagree. It is a perfectly fair and very often effective question if used properly. I admit you can't always start the sale with too many but most of the time it's a great way to close the sale. Some additional responses may be, "If we could find a vehicle that you liked, would you have the time to take a test drive today?" or "If we could get your monthly investment to that figure, would you be in a position to own it today?"

Do not be shy when you are in the proper situation to return a question to influence a commitment. This is one of your best opportunities to gain the commitment you need to make the sale. It is here that you have leverage. Take the opportunity they have given and have them consider your agreement as a condition of the sale. This will better allow our customers to commit and will often help in completing each step in the process. It is effective at slowing the fast-paced customer and helping indecisive customers take action.

Of course, it is also important to keep in mind the old saying, "It is not what you say, but how you say it." It is here that you may want to vary how serious or light your presentation is depending on where your level of rapport is currently at. You may want to soften your approach in some circumstances. Always note the timing and the response of your delivery. Then again, at other times, like in the final stages of closing, you may want to remain straight and serious while seeking your question-based commitments. Some of our customers, depending on their buying processes, may be quite elusive when committing to the final terms. With some, leveraging a commitment may be the only definitive way to initiate a sale. Different customers will often require different actions. You want to gain the mini-commitments needed to make the sale and yet still be aware of their willingness to participate. Think of questioning as an act of measured balance. Maintain your forward direction by varying your encouragement with a catered amount of apprehension relief.

FINAL NOTE

Sales is not a career where a reserved or inhibited person will succeed. Your customers will not likely present you with all the information you need to make a sale. You will often have to investigate your customer's needs and then lead them with their own answers.

If you ever had a customer say, "Okay, well, thank you for all your help and information," it is likely that he or she was the one asking the questions. It is also likely that a sale did not occur. Do not let this happen to you. Ask the proper questions at the appropriate times and lead your customer through the steps of the sale. You can't just tell your customers what car they should buy, but you can absolutely ask them what kind of car they would like. Know your customer, know your plan, and always believe that the person asking the questions chooses the path and the direction in each step of the sale.

13

READING PEOPLE

How we best understand someone is by the answers to the questions we ask. However, sometimes people's thoughts, emotions, and concerns will not be readily evident in their answers alone. They may only come out in their facial expression, body language, or tone of voice. It is this nonverbal language that we will be learning how to observe here. It is through this language that we will develop our sense of understanding.

The purpose of our understanding is to gain an overall image of our customer's personality and emotions, so we will know how best to interact with each. Our customer's expressions and mannerisms, defined from our observations, will often give us an accurate picture on how to best communicate. The purpose of this chapter is to learn how to quickly and accurately read our customers.

AWARENESS

Would you communicate with your friends from back home differently than you would with your child's teacher? Do people interact differently at a backyard barbeque than they would at an opera?

The answers to these questions should be easy because of the disparity of the scenes. However in a sales setting it will be a little more difficult to understand the preferred style of your customer because you will be meeting them out of their typical environment. You must rely on the clues available. Your ability to quickly read people and adjust your approach to best line up with their individual presence and preferred style of interaction is essential. This is why we must raise our level of perception through our skill of observation.

PEOPLE SKILLS

There are three key factors involving the people we meet that we will learn about for our understanding. They are our customer's personal style, their individual emotions, and their overall personality. Our early goal is to recognize each factor and understand how they relate in our interaction..

PERSONAL STYLE

One's personal style is what he or she has chosen to be in the world. It is the environment they have chosen to exist and how they have adapted to fit. It is their job, their home, their dress, their choice of activities, and the people they associate with. It is how and where they feel comfortable.

Understanding your customers style is important to help determine common ground and build rapport. This is the information needed to help provide a level of comfort. For example, the style you would want to use while interacting with a priest, a construction worker, and a business executive will all vary. To become a top salesperson, you have to be able to work successfully with a diverse range of customers.

INDIVIDUAL EMOTIONS

Your customer's emotions are the unique thoughts or feelings they may have and will typically exhibit through their physical language. Some examples may be boredom, excitement, attentiveness, or anxiety. Note that some of these are helpful in selling a vehicle and some are not. It is important to recognize our customer's emotions so we can quickly work to encourage or diffuse the varying ones.

By understanding our customer's more inherent set of actions and reactions, we will better know when and to what level we should react to the emotions that appear. The emotions we can't change, we should seek to adapt to, and the ones we can, we should look to do so to create a more positive sales setting. A quick example would be to calm an angry customer or involve an inattentive customer.

PERSONALITY

One's personality is the totality of their behavioral and emotional characteristics. It is how someone both chooses to and reflexively acts and reacts in a setting. It is a person's complete image, influenced by their temperament, disposition, and behavioral style. It is their overall behavioral pattern.

It is this personality that we will have to be able to understand and work with to excel as salespeople. To help accomplish this, we must prepare ourselves to understand the people we will meet from the clues that are available.

OBSERVATION

By recognizing our customer's personal style, we are better able to accommodate them and make them comfortable. By recognizing their individual emotions, we are better equipped to help maintain the sales forward direction by reacting with the proper responses. By understanding their overall personality, we can best know what traits to expect and prepare ourselves to adapt and respond appropriately.

Salespeople who excel in these areas have become skillful in the act of observation. By closely observing people's actions, we are often able to read the active and subconscious messages that our customers will send. In the first step of the process, we will use our observations to establish a proper greeting and help develop common ground. In each of the following steps, we will continue to observe and analyze our customer's presence to give us the guidance we need to keep the process moving forward.

GETTING STARTED

To help get yourself going, start paying more attention to people. Think about what you're seeing and hearing. Start with a blank chart and an open mind. Involve all of your senses. Gather information about the people you are observing to gain clues on the type of people they are.

How someone dresses, what someone drives, and the jewelry one wears can all give you insight to help establish the person your customer might be. Ask yourself; are these items a possible reflection of their style? Take your observations and combine them with their body language, verbal tone, and mannerisms for an overall picture. Try to recognize the similarities that may be present. See if you can combine your customer's overall appearance and actions to help form a starting image of their personality type.

ONE'S CHOSEN APPEARANCE

While you cannot definitively state that a person is conservative, flashy, or carefree by the car they drive or the clothes they wear, these characteristics may certainly be clues to their overall image.

Do flashy clothes indicate an outgoing personality? Does a conservative dresser indicate a more reserved person? Does a cluttered car indicate a busy person?

Not necessarily, but when taken in combination of their actions, they can certainly give you an idea of how to calculate relating character traits to help determine how best to interact. The key to bringing the overall picture into better focus is to continue adding to your information as your interaction progresses.

Would you greet an outgoing person differently than you would a reserved person? Would you be more direct and informative when presenting to a busy person?

Although there is no perfect answer and this isn't an exact science, your observations and ability to read someone quickly is helpful early on in your interaction and throughout your meeting. As your communication increases and your customer's style becomes more evident, simply adjust your presence to theirs.

THEIR TRADE-IN

The vehicle your customer is currently driving will often offer you a host of insight. The color, size, and style are just some of the clues available. How your customer has chosen to accessorize their vehicle may also further aid in your quest. Let your curiosity and inquisitiveness take over.

Does their vehicle have personalized license plates? How about an alarm? What is the sound system like? Is there a bumper sticker or a club association sticker on the bumper or windshield? How has it been maintained? Is it old, new, expensive, economical, or flashy?

Take the answers to these questions and match them with the traits that were common in previous experiences. Recognize your potential in gaining the common ground and insight on how best to communicate.

For example, might there be a style difference between the person who has a bike rack and the person who has a ladder rack? Would these people typically have different interests? Can we use the clues we obtain in our observations to help us realize their interests and gain common ground? Is common ground important in building rapport?

Again, the common answer here, in most cases, is likely to be yes. A person's choice of possessions and accessories are often a good indication of their preferred style and personality, and are also possible topics of conversation.

PLACE OF EMPLOYMENT AND RESIDENCE

The environment that your customers choose to exist is also an extension of their personality. The type of work a person does and where someone chooses to live will often give you an example of certain preferences or acquired traits he or she may have.

Would a production foreman be less leisurely when selecting a vehicle than an artist? Would an engineer more likely need logical reasons to justify their purchase? Would a financial advisor be more concerned than most with the investment required in their choice?

Although you cannot conclude a particular buyer's style with this source alone, you should be able to use this information to become further aware of how your customers will likely conduct themselves.

Where people choose to live is another example of the atmosphere they may find comfortable. Your customers driver's license or registration card is needed for test drives or appraisals, so this information is readily available.

Learn where your customers live and learn about where they live. Do they live in a gated community, an industrial town, the inner city, the suburbs, or the country? Has the influence of their neighborhood adjusted the way they see, approach, or interact with people? Could this influence adjust their level of outgoingness?

Do not ignore the signs that are readily available. Understanding your customer's chosen community will often give you the information needed to help better relate to them. Always take every advantage you can to help you better understand and relate to your customers.

THEIR FRIENDS

If your customers come in with another person, maybe a friend or a relative, pay attention to how they interact. This may give you the best example of the style in which they prefer to communicate. Try to recognize the patterns of their mannerisms and emotions.

Are their children with them? How do they relate with them? How people's children act in public is often a good indication of their expectations of others. This might be a beneficial guide for how to adjust your own level of professionalism when enacting your process.

COMMUNICATION

Learn to focus on a person's voice when they are speaking. Understand that in many cases, it is not what people say that conveys their true message, but how they say it. Where people put an emphasis in the sentence, the pitch of their tone, and the rate of their speech will all give you insight to their thoughts and intentions.

There are many messages that people knowingly and unknowingly send when communicating. Determine if there is motive in their voice. Are they aware they are altering their tone or is it a result of the emotions they are feeling? Add the context of each situation and the variations of their expressions to help answer your questions.

Does a loud voice indicate someone who needs to be in control? Does fast talking indicate nervousness or anxiety?

INCREASE YOUR EXPOSURE

The fastest way to increase your ability to observe is to do just that, observe. Start watching people. The more people watching you do, the more information you will have to rely on. Think of this as building your information file. The more data you have to draw from, the more likely you will know how to proceed. Go out into the world where people gather, and prepare to observe. Focus on people's actions, mannerisms, and speech, and try to think of the emotions they are feeling and the personalities they have. This is enlightening. People watching can also be fun. Treat it like a competition.

See how often you can accurately gauge someone's next move by watching his or her previous one. Keep watching. Once you can consistently anticipate a person's next move, you will be well on your way to selling more cars.

Please believe that this is not more than is needed to sell a car. In fact, your perception and the ability to quickly read people is exactly what is needed. If you can envision a typical response to an action or reaction, you will be more likely to succeed in influencing or persuading their responses and actions. Our ability to observe is the source we must draw from while creating the actions and questions that will produce the responses we are seeking.

FINE-TUNE YOUR ABILITY

Some additional settings to further your people-reading skills are places where a commissioned sale may take place. Some examples may be an electronics store, an appliance center, a furniture showroom, or a franchised clothing store. When you are at work or in another place of business, put yourself in training mode. Learn from the interactions that are taking place. Learn from others. Many times, when you are personally involved in a sale, it is hard to be an objective learner. Your own involvement or anxiety will cloud your ability to observe objectively.

While watching and listening to customers milling around the products, see if you can gain some insight into their style and formulate an approach comfortable for them. Watch and listen to their expressions, mannerisms, and voice inflections. How were they approached, and how did they respond? Were you accurate in your estimation? Was the salesperson? How would you have adjusted your own selling style to better complement the customer's likely preferred style? Continue to observe. Watch for the patterns of their reactions. Remember, the ability to read people effectively requires the constant and continued perception and understanding of every sound or move one may make.

SENSE OF FEELING

Have you ever thought a certain way but just couldn't explain it, or had a feeling about something but couldn't put a finger on it? Well, this was probably your subconscious telling you something.

During the course of everyday life, too much happens for us to be able to absorb all that we see in our conscious memory. Much of it gets put away in our subconscious. As we observe, our subconscious memories are filled with random pictures that will often help guide us in the future. We begin to create an internal file of information that allows us to start assessing accurate views almost instinctively. This is called our intuition. Our intuition is a powerful tool to have in guiding our actions and a large reason why we should always look to increase our exposure in observing people.

When working with your customers, you might not see or recognize all the signs, however, you will often get a sense of their varying feelings. Well, if you do, this may be a time that you should pay attention. When you have a sense of uncertainty, seek to investigate. If you have a sense of interest, continue your path. Do not let your sales relationships take the wrong turn or miss your opportunities. Always seek to understand and adjust your actions as best suited. Sometimes your awareness and concern will in itself help to encourage a more comfortable selling atmosphere.

REFINE YOUR OWN GROUPS

To continue developing our people skills, we will soon be taking a look at our customers emotions and some buying personalities. This is to further our ability in recognizing the differences in the people we meet and identify future actions and reactions. However, know there is no set standard here. There really can't be because of all the variations possible. There are no rights or wrongs. This being the case, much of your learning must come from your own experiences.. The more you expand your abilities, the more experience you can draw from. The further you refine your profiles, the more accurate you will be in relating to the people you meet. Emotion and personality headings are not important. What is important is to actively develop a means to better relate to and interact with the people you will be meeting.

FINAL NOTE

Have you ever heard someone described as having a unique ability to connect with others? It can't be explained, but people just seem to naturally take a liking to them? Well, I think this is the essence of this chapter.

People skills are important. They are important in our regular everyday life and they are important in our profession. Do not let someone tell you that they are not. Sales is not just presenting an item, it is understanding how to best present an item. Sales is a creation of balance between you and your customer. It is a harmony that is created by your ability to act and react to each physical and emotional move your customer may make. It is having the advanced ability to observe, understand, and adapt to people in a way that instantly creates a rhythm or harmony.

Yes, to be successful in sales requires you to have more than one skill and a deeper level of understanding than most. However, please believe this understanding is achievable and these skills are attainable. In fact, most of what is needed to be successful can be reached by nothing more than your desire to be successful and an open mind. Start now and seek to develop your sense of understanding. Create the ability to interact with each of your customers in a manner that is most beneficial to each.

14

WHY A CUSTOMER BUYS

A person will buy when he or she feels a solution has been found for his or her wants or needs. People will make a purchase when they feel that they have found a product that will somehow make their lives better. Buying a vehicle is like any other purchasing decision one may make. Your customers want the luxury, safety, status, or mileage they feel their selection will provide.

A person's decision to purchase a vehicle is often a result of the influence in which they have allowed themselves to be persuaded. The exact point of this decision is reached when they have found a vehicle that will satisfy their objectives, and when they feel its value is equal to the investment required.

VALUE

As salespeople, we must understand that the key word here is value. This is because the definition of value is one of perception and is always open to outside influence. In sales, it is this perception of value that will be the driving factor in your customer's decision-making process.

Understanding this enables you to realize that the key role you, the salesperson, will have is to build the value needed to influence a purchase. It allows you to realize that it is you, who is in the best position to influence the customer's selection and persuade them to make a decision.

WHAT MOTIVATES A PURCHASE

In order to best influence our customers in purchasing, we must first recognize their motivating factors and learn to build upon each one. It is these motivating factors that will help initiate a purchase if we are able to identify, support, and confirm how each will help to encourage a decision.

EMOTION

Most customers will start out driven by specific wants and needs, and will often have very determined parameters set up for themselves. They will try to make a logical decision based strictly on the facts of the vehicle and the cost involved in purchasing. However, in large purchases such as a new vehicle, there are often additional factors in how someone will ultimately decide to purchase. Many will also be influenced by the experience that you are able to provide and their consequent emotions at the time.

The thought of owning a new or newer vehicle can be exciting, even for the most conservative. Your customer's emotions, combined with the feelings that occur as a result of their experience, will often sway their decision as much as the vehicle or price in question. This being the case, much of your efforts should be centered on your customer's emotional wants and needs, as these are what will most often determine their final action.

Make no mistake, people will alter what they buy, where they buy, and from whom they buy, all as a result of their emotions at the time. This is why it is so important to follow the steps that will best allow us to be in a position of influence. This is why it's so important to provide a positive atmosphere and a comfortable experience. You must take the time to build rapport, ask credible questions, and listen intently to your customer's wants and needs. You must follow and complete each persuasion-building step of the sales process.

PERSUASION

Some will drive across the state to save a few dollars, and some will gladly pay more to do business closer. However, either could probably have been persuaded to do the opposite. There is no right or wrong answer in buying a car. What, when, why, and from whom someone buys are all open to influence. It's all a matter of perception, which is controlled by the specific emotion at the exact time of each decision.

Please know if your customers like you, trust you, and feel comfortable in working with you, they will almost always be open to your advice. Do not doubt this, this is true. Think about how many times you went out to purchase a particular product and came back with something you liked better after listening to the advice of others. It is you; the salesperson, who can help alter, shape, and form their decisions. Your customers will allow you to persuade them if your influence is credible and well received.

People themselves know that they are not always fully in control of their own emotions when making a decision. This is one of the reasons many will state they are, "just looking", upon entering your store. They know they are receptive to persuasion and may not yet want to be asked to make a decision before having a chance to form an opinion on their own. Many will want some time to get a feel for you and your dealership before stating their intentions. However, with the proper approach, do not ever assume that your customers will not be receptive to your open, honest, and credible advice. In fact, it is your job to use the knowledge and experience you have to help your customers make the decisions that are right for them. Once you have assessed their needs and determined the vehicle that is most suited to them, you owe it to them to be persuasive and persistent in your motivating efforts.

ATTENTION TO DETAILS

All top salespeople understand that there are often many vehicles that will satisfy a given person's needs. This being the case, it only stands to reason that most buying decisions are made for smaller, less tangible reasons.

To be completely successful, you must understand that each person you work with will in some way be more or less influenced by every action or reaction that occurs. Your customers may like your service department, your location, your presentation, or your dealerships hours. Equally, they may dislike all of these things about you or your dealership. All of these factors and more will be scored consciously or subconsciously as pluses and minuses in your customer's decision-making process. For this reason, you must observe your customer's actions and emotions for the subtle hints that will help guide you in giving them comfort. You must look to encourage your customer's positive emotions and buffer or soften their negative emotions in each step of the process.

UNDERSTANDING WANTS AND NEEDS

The initial factors in our customer's reasoning to purchase are their wants and their needs. Earlier, we looked into the importance of setting ourselves up to be persuasive in our interaction. Now let's take a look at understanding our customer's early motivations. It is important to understand our customer's wants and needs so we will better know how to increase their desires and perception of value.

A customers need is recognized as a logical desire where their wants are more emotionally driven, A persons needs are usually more predetermined or set and their wants are more created and subjected to influence. Again note that many vehicles may satisfy a persons needs. A need or perceived need may be the reason that people will initiate their search, but it is usually their wants that will decide when they take action. Most considerable purchases are emotionally driven. Please understand, a person will pay more and decide quicker if they are excited about their pending solution.

NEEDS

A need is the result of an event that necessitates an action. It may be that someone's vehicle has been damaged, stolen, broken down, or is in some way unavailable. It may also be that their current vehicle no longer suits their transportation needs. Perhaps their family is growing and they need more room, or a longer trip to work necessitates better mileage. Knowing your customer's needs will better enable you to help select the vehicle that will solve their problems. It will give you the information needed to help logically persuade them.

LATENT NEEDS

Latent needs are needs not yet realized by your customer. For example, your customer may have a vehicle worn to the point that it will require attention soon. Although they may not have recognized it yet, they have an impending need, and the age and mileage of the car may not justify repairing it. It could be in their best financial interest to make a move now, while their vehicle still has a respectable trade value.

A top salesperson will search for impending needs and develop them into buying motives. All vehicles need maintenance and will eventually need repairs. This customer's motive would be to lessen financial risk and increase peace of mind. To help uncover your customer's future needs, ask the questions that will offer them the opportunity to see the possibilities.

WANTS

A person's wants are the feelings that are created in anticipation of attaining an objective. It is what will ultimately drive one to acquire what he or she wishes to have. It is your customer's wants that will be the driving factor behind most of their vehicle purchases.

Understand that your customer's level of desire will always be either increased or decreased by the influences or actions that occur during your sales interaction. It is because of this that you must become skilled in recognizing and building upon your customer's wants and create an experience that will help aid your influence. It is their wants that will allow you to create the energy and excitement needed to keep their forward direction to the sale. A person will pay more and decide quicker if they are excited about their choice.

INITIATIVE TO BUY

In order to best prepare to be in a position of influence, we must often adapt our initial approach to what will best be received by our individual customers. Even though our customers will often be swayed by the emotions that occur while involved in the experience we provide, it is important to recognize their early motivational factors to know how best to interact with each in the early stages of our meeting.

The most influential factor for us to understand here is want versus need. Understand that different people will often be more motivated by different levels of each.

People who are conditioned to think in a structured type environment may initially respond only to logic. This is because their patterns of thought are likely to be influenced by their environment and similarly structured. With these customers, you are usually best advised to initially present only the information you feel will guide them to best rationalize a decision. Humor, excitement, and sizzle, will often not be helpful in the early stages of your meeting.

158

With other customers however, like those who are less structured, a more emotional approach may be better suited.

To help establish your ability to connect with each, try to determine the dominant motivation they have in visiting. If they are initially needoriented, start by addressing their needs. If they are initially wantoriented, start by addressing their wants. Then, as your sales relationship progresses, decide how much attention to spend on each to help further your connection. Their level of resolve of each, possibly varying at different stages in the process, is where you should direct your efforts.

Understand that the path of your customer's eventual decision will only evolve in the direction of your influence if you are able to successfully open their receptiveness and maintain it throughout your interaction. In the beginning, know you will often have to get close enough to their pattern of thought before they'll start to open up and become receptive.

WHAT A CUSTOMER WANTS IN A VEHICLE

What a customer wants in a vehicle will vary from person to person. Each will have his or her own set of benefits that he or she will seek to attain. It is here that you will have to know your vehicle's options and their benefits. You will also need to understand how your customers will view each benefit as it relates to the wants they are looking to acquire.

Here is a list. Notice that some of these will motivate you personally to purchase and some will not. The purpose of this is for you to become aware of other people's motivational factors, not your own. As you read each one, try to imagine how they may appeal to your differing customers and create a strategy to build upon the desire of each.

- Safety   Luxury   • Status
- Exclusivity   •Style   • Comfort

- Power
- Fuel economy
- Performance
- Performance

- Warranty
- Reliability
- Time-tested
- Reliability

- Agility
- Low maintenance
- Passenger capacity
- Time Tested

Whether they perceive it as a want or a need, most customers will have some central motive when settling on a vehicle. It's probably one of the factors listed here. Use your customer's main motivating factor as the focus point for your persuasive efforts. When your customers inquire about a specific vehicle, relate back to the reasoning others shared when showing an interest in that vehicle and what prompted their interest. Determine your customer's initial interest and seek to understand how they were influenced.

Some additional insight may be in how your individual vehicles are marketed. The manufacturer's ads on television, in magazines, and in newspapers will often present the image they want their vehicles to produce. Your trucks may be tough, your compacts may be economical, your sedans may be luxurious, and your vans may be spacious. Become aware of the key words and slogans that your manufacturers use as it's often these motivations that will encourage your customers to buy.

If the safety of a vehicle is most important to your customer, focus on how your vehicle is safe. Explain the crumple zones, the side air-bags, the safety canopy, the side door beams, the transverse mounted engine, etc. Concentrate on presenting the features of that particular desire. Do not center your focus or concentrate on features of the vehicle in which they have not developed an interest.

WHAT A CUSTOMER WANTS FROM A SALESPERSON

People want a salesperson who is attuned to their needs, capable of speaking to them on their level, and is respectful and accommodating to their preferred style of comfort. They want a salesperson who projects an open manner, is sensitive to other's personalities, and who knows how best to adapt with their own. They want a salesperson who will listen to their wants and needs, and then cater a presentation just for them.

Make no mistake; the more positive their experience is with you, the more likely they will buy from you.

- Honest
- Credible
- Trustworthy

- Likeable
- Informative
- Unique

- Knowledgeable
- Sense of Humor
- Pleasing personality

At some level, people know that they will somehow tie their future ownership experience in with their purchasing experience on big-ticket items, such as cars. Thus, your customers may consciously or subconsciously proceed or defer from making a purchasing decision based upon the experience you provide. If they're incurring a bad experience, they may avoid purchasing a vehicle. Conversely, if they're having a good experience, they may be more likely to purchase in order to additionally create the pleasant future memories that will begin every time they drive their new car. In any case, do not doubt the power of a positive experience.

BUYING SIGNALS

Buying signals are the signs that your customers will display when they are moving toward making a purchase. When your customers exhibit the signs of wanting to move forward, it is usually preceded by a recent event or occurrence of events that initiated an increased desire. This action or series of events is often a direct indication of why your particular customer seeks to buy. It is important to recognize their buying signals so we will know where and to what degree certain motivations exist when helping to confirm their selection and increasing their desire.

- Smiling and leaning forward with intent

- Wanting to clarify certain information

- Asking about financing or payment options

- Asking about the time needed to complete the paperwork

- Portraying how they will enjoy their new vehicle

- Asking questions about your service department

- Looking at members of their party to test or confirm their level of interest

It is also important to take notice of your customer's signs so you will know when they are willing to move forward. Timing is important. If you ask for the sale too early, your customers may deem you too forward and back off. Similarly, if you wait too long, their buying desire may diminish. Learn to monitor your customer's emotions and then react to them. Act when their levels of receptivity and desire are at their highest. Seek to encourage their positive feelings and diffuse their negative ones. Learn to recognize your customer's signs of interest, build upon their desires, and then take the initiative to ask for the sale as their level of interest builds.

HOW CUSTOMERS BUY

How people decide is likely to be by the process in which they were shaped. Please understand the importance of this. Our process is our guide. It is the reason that we will likely arrive at our intended destination. In order to best aid in the experience that we are able to provide, we must have a format that will help smooth our customer's transition from customers to owners, from unsure to enthusiastic.

Our process is the best template for any path. Although adaptable in its use, its consistency in form will provide our best approach in constructing a decision. To help further the understanding of our process's steps, let's take a look at an example of a simple everyday occurrence; say, selecting a movie. Let's separate each step, and see how easily each can be incorporated into our process to help provide the structure in achieving our goal.

When seeking to select a movie of choice; we will greet our intended guest, present our selection for consideration, build value in our choice, ask for their agreement, overcome their objections, and ultimately enjoy the show. Each bit of influence, no matter how simple or common, is always best achieved by a process. It is how someone is best influenced to "buy." Although the process of the sale may not perfectly align with each decision you seek, its basic structure will always provide your best path of influence.

Understand that most decisions are externally formed. If you think about it, this makes sense. Even when we seem to come up with something on our own, it is still likely that we were influenced. Whether by society, culture, schooling, or our jobs, our whole world is shaped by outside influences. As soon as our parents brought us home, whether through reward or penalty, our conditioning will likely have begun. We do something because it is expected. We wake up at similar times, put on similar clothes, take similar forms of transportation, and complete similar tasks. For as many different people we have in our country, think how many are so, so similar. Wife, husband, 2.5 kids, etc. The structure of our society is based on conformity. We watch the majority and adjust to fit. We follow the process.

Please understand the relevance of this. Learn the process, understand the process, and believe in the process. A person's desires, motivations, enthusiasm and actions are all subject to influence. As long as you are able to present your customer with a comfortable experience and atmosphere, your process will absolutely provide the path he or she will gladly follow.

WHY CUSTOMERS DON'T BUY

Why customers buy is because they have found a solution to their wants or needs. However, their final agreement must also be accompanied by a resolution of their concerns and uncertainties. To help further understand why our customers buy, we must also realize some of the many reasons they choose not to buy. When we can recognize and understand this reasoning, we can then look to offer the new information needed to change the direction of their decision.

The customers that choose not to buy are in some way unable to justify a forward move. For some reason, they have created a blocking force that is keeping them from buying.

Fear of the wrong vehicle, fear of not getting a good deal, not sure of their wants, no hurry, no perceived need, has a better deal, fear of what others will think, no value, no trust and just plain old feeling uncomfortable, are some of the objections we will face.

People's concerns and objections will often follow a general guide. However, there will always be the variances and uniqueness in each. Some of your customer's reasons for not purchasing may be hard to recognize. To help foresee and understand your customer's potential reasons, you will often have to actively monitor their actions and emotions for the level of interest and commitment they have. If you feel a concern has appeared, try to back up to the moment your feeling started to occur.

Understand it is not as simple as whether your customers like your car or not. At any time, a hesitancy may occur. However, also understand, although a specific circumstance may temporarily sway your customer's forward direction, please know they will often accept a remedy and move forward if you are able to recognize and satisfy their concern. It's usually the sum of their total experience that will precipitate a final move in one direction or another. It is the whole experience that they will be evaluating for a purchase of this size. As a salesperson, you have to understand and trust this. If you have found your customer's ideal vehicle, you should be informative, persuasive, and persistent in confirming their choice and overcoming their objections.

WHY YOUR CUSTOMER WILL BUY

The real purpose of this chapter and a major part of this book is to understand why your particular customer will buy. It is to understand how best to work with and adjust to each of the people you will meet.

Understand that a person's wants, needs, level of desire and sense of value are all contributing factors to their eventual decision. However there will always be the factors that are unique to the individual and situation in which you are involved. Each person you work with will have his or her differing means in enacting a decision and will have their own unique best path in accepting our influence. It is for this reason you must become skillful in observing and reading the people you will meet.

How is it that your customer will choose to act? Is their goal to get a price and leave for the next company? Will a past experience affect their future with you? Will their opening personality have them follow your lead or question your every move? Will they want to sleep on their decision? Will your price be too high? What will be the final factor in how they will buy? Will it align with their initial intention?

Recognize that there is no standard in ones forming of a decision. Recognize also that you must not use your own buying habits or style of comfort as a template for how or why a person will act. Our response is always dependent upon their created presence. The reason that we adapt to our customers is to better connect and ultimately better create our level of influence. We adapt to their personality so they will better adapt to our process.

FINAL NOTE

The biggest influence in a person's decision to buy is how good an experience the salesperson is able to provide. If a customer likes their salesperson, trusts their advice, and is comfortable with their level of service, they will make every attempt to buy from them. The customer will select and purchase their most likely choice. There will always be the factors that are not in our control, however, they will always be those that are.

Please understand this; customers will buy the salesperson before they will buy what is being offered. All successful salespeople know this, all failing salespeople do not want to believe this. This is why one person in your dealership will consistently sell above the average, and others will consistently sell below. The exciting part to recognize here however, is that with the proper skills and learning ability, anyone can perform at the higher level.

15

RECOGNIZING THE SIGNS

Think of your drive to work in the morning. Try and visualize all of the devices that keep you headed in the right direction. There are lanes, curbs, and an assortment of signs and signals that lead the way. In order for you to arrive at work, you need to know when to steer left or right, when to slow down, and when to speed up. You rely on being able to understand the signs and signals to help reach your destination. Now imagine you didn't notice the signs or were unable to read them. Would you easily find your way?

It is the same when you are trying to sell a car. If you do not recognize the signs or signals your customers are sending, you will be less likely to sell them a vehicle. Many times, when you were unable to sell a car and couldn't understand why, you were probably missing the signals your customers were providing. However, by developing your ability to observe people's actions and read their conscious and subconscious messages, you will be better prepared to keep your customers on the right path.

YOUR UNDERSTANDING

The importance of our customers signals lies in the emotions that prompted their emergence. As a salesperson, it is our goal to read and interpret the signs and signals that our customers provide, so that we are better able to recognize their emotions and effectively react to each. Earlier we increased our level of observation and developed an understanding of how it will aid our success. Let's now focus on recognizing and responding to some of the specific emotions that we will soon be presented with in our profession.

In sales, there are both positive and negative emotions that will occur. Some negative emotions may be boredom, frustration, confusion, or impatience. Some positive ones may be attentiveness, excitement, or interest. To be successful, it is our goal to encourage our customers positive emotions and diffuse their negative ones.. This is how we will both control the path of the process and keep its forward momentum. However, before we will be able to respond accurately to any of our customer's varying emotions, we must first be able to recognize the signs that indicate an emotion exists.

The most effective way to respond appropriately is with a set plan of approach. Observe, analyze, understand, and react. You *observe* the signals they send, *analyze* them for the emotion involved, *understand* why the emotion occurred, and *react* appropriately. To perform this sequence effectively, we must always be vigilant and perceptive. As salespeople, we must act as emotion screeners. We must be able to encourage, shape, dissuade, or diffuse each emotion to keep our customers on the correct path.

EMOTIONS: THE SIGNS AND SOLUTIONS

A customer's non-verbal language is a large part of their communication and often a telling sign of their true feelings. People can choose what they will say, but it is hard to disguise the immediate signs of an emotion that will come out in their expressions and movements. These are usually reflex reactions and are more often than not quite genuine.

To help recognize the signs and emotions you may come across, I have included the more prominent ones here. To start, read through the list and try to picture them in your past. Then, pay close attention in your future interactions and match the varying emotions with the signals you see. The more people you interact with, the more aware

168

you will become of the predictable relation between a person's outward presence and his or her corresponding internal thoughts.

Before we begin, please note the difference between an emotion and a personality type. An emotion is a reaction to a specific cause, whereas a personality type is more of a recurring theme. Adjusting to one's personality is a continued, flexible state of complementation, where an emotion may require immediate and direct attention.

SOME COMMON EMOTIONS

DOUBTFUL

Possible signs: focused eyes, squinting, tilted head, one eyebrow higher than the other.

Solution: Seek to verify the facts. Back up to your most recent statement and offer verifying data. Support your presentation with information that will clarify your customer's doubt. If unsure of their reason for doubt, ask if there is something they are unsure of or if they have any questions. Try to measure your interaction and seek feedback. Search out their reasoning and answer it. You cannot move forward until this is resolved. Credibility is crucial in sales.

BORED

Possible signs: sighing, wandering eyes, twiddling, yawning, stretching, shifting positions, rocking, looking at watch.

Solution: Involve the customer. Stop talking and seek to include them in your presentation. Try some involvement questions or physical activity. Listen to their responses and further their input. Engage them. Turn up the enthusiasm. Enough of the facts; involve their emotions.

FRUSTRATED

Possible signs: exaggerated moves, hand gesturing, shrugging shoulders, repeating themselves.

Solution: Frustration is usually the result of another emotion that was either not recognized or not acknowledged. Seek to identify and alleviate the issue. Try to backtrack and determine the cause. Once you have found the origin, diffuse the customer's frustration directly by solving or clarifying their issue or concern. If you cannot diffuse it completely, try to lighten it or divert their attention. Take them visually back to a place they enjoy. The longer this emotion exists, the worse it will get. Seek to understand the source and immediately amend it.

INATTENTIVE

Possible signs: lack of eye contact, swaying, diverted focus.

Solution: Your customers may be preoccupied or losing interest. Seek to determine their source of preoccupation. If it's just that they are losing interest, involve them with some open-ended questions. Try to energize them. Turn up the volume on your show. If they're preoccupied and its source is other than you, try to determine what it is and show empathy and compassion. Put yourself in your customer's position and seek to understand its significance. It may be best to reschedule, depending on the effect their distraction is having. Use your best judgment. If you have to reschedule, always be sure to follow up.

IMPATIENT

Possible signs: heavy sighing, aggressive watch looking, shifting quickly from side-to-side, turning flush.

Solution: Stop the process and gain the customer's attention. Apologize for the pace and provide an immediate course of action. This way, the customer will see the progression as it takes place. Impatience is often caused by uncertainty. Chart your agenda completely and assure the customer that you will be moving forward. You may even quicken your tempo here. However, do not let your customers force you to skip the steps of the sales process. You are always more likely to make a sale by following the process.

ANXIOUS/NERVOUS

Possible signs: erratic movements, pacing, fidgeting, tapping, hand-wringing.

Solution: Try to take your customer's thoughts to a different place. Provide a mental image of a place they enjoy. Guide the conversation back to one of the activities, experiences, or associations that you learned about in your rapport-building stage. Engage in small talk. Revisit the common ground you have established. Get them to talk about themselves and what they enjoy.

DEFENSIVE

Possible signs: arms folded, mouth closed, backed into a stable stance.

Solution: Defensiveness is usually a direct result of the manner of your questioning or interaction. Ease up on the degree of your intensity. Back off a little. Use a more empathetic approach. Seek to develop a thoughtful or more caring manner. When questioning, formulate a softer, less repetitive style.

CONFUSED

Possible signs: hand to forehead, focused look, repeating movements, hand through the hair.

Solution: Clear up the point of issue. Try to narrow the scope of your presentation by eliminating the items of least importance or concern. Identify the source of the issue and then seek to analyze and clarify it. Explain your position in a clear manner. Separate relative issues and provide understanding for each.

INSULTED

Possible signs: focused look, head moved back, pointed eyes.

Solution: Some people are touchier than others. If you accidentally insult someone, ease off quickly. Depending on the context of the situation, you have one of two choices in proceeding. The first option is to try to laugh it off as if you were kidding. If you choose this option, try to react quickly with a joke aimed at yourself to sort of balance it out. Self-directed humor will usually help defer most negative feelings the customer may have felt as a result of a misinterpreted action. If successful, act as if they are good sports. Keep the situation as light as possible. The second option is to apologize. Take full blame for your miscalculation and assure them you meant no ill will. Note that you will probably have to convince them it was not your intention to offend them before they will be receptive to you continuing.

EVASIVE

Possible signs: looking away, facing in another direction, less communication.

Solution: Your customers are either hiding something or feel that moving forward will uncover something. This may be a response to a direct question or a result of something they foresee in the future. In either case, you should make no notice of it or investigate it, depending on its relevance or importance. If questioning the customer will not scare them away, search or question for the reason why. One example would be the avoidance of something they think of as embarrassing, such as not yet having a down payment.

Try to determine the reason without putting the customer on the spot. Use the context of the situation. Be sure to vary your investigative approach to balance the level of anxiety they have. Be careful in your search. Once you've determined the source of evasiveness, either show understanding or move on quickly, depending on the situation. If people are embarrassed, they will usually look for the exit, so quickly re-engage them in another topic after initiating your best response. Note that this emotion will usually hinder your ability to move forward to a sale until it is resolved.

GUILTY/ CAUGHT IN LIE

Possible signs: looking down or away, turning flush, talking fast, hand over mouth, looking for the nearest exit. Similar to being evasive.

172

Solutions: Be careful not to press too hard here or overemphasize that you caught them. Your goal is to sell a car, not to prove you're right. Most people need credibility. Try to change the subject. If the lie is really obvious or is a conversation stopper, admit your own mistakes or fibs. See if admitting some of your own miscalculations will help diffuse your customer's discomfort. If you need to, try admiring their technique. Laugh it off. Remember, if you embarrass them, they will probably want to hide or leave.

INDECISIVE

Possible signs: moving or looking back and forth, tilting head side-to-side, focusing and un-focusing.

Solution: Separate the issues and try to clarify the points. Help weigh the positives and negatives of each choice. Evaluate the situation, determine the best response, and then seek to influence a resolution. Do not be too aggressive in the decisions you deem beneficial. The customer may become skeptical of your motives. Portray both sides, while presenting the most beneficial side with a little more eloquence.

AGITATED

Possible signs: becoming stiff, turning red, aggressive movements, tenseness.

Solutions: Seek to calm the customer. Determine the source of their agitation and eliminate or explain it in a compassionate manner. This will often separate the customer from their current thoughts and help them to relax. Offer a soda or drink. Ask if there is anything you can do for them. Try to recognize the reason for their uneasiness and resolve it before reentering the sales process. Once the situation has been successfully diffused, move on and avoid its return.

REACT PROMPTLY

When something comes up that you deem out of place with the usual character of your customer, you should take notice.

These are probably emotions that you should address. If, in the course of your presentation, your customer shows signs of boredom or lack of attentiveness and these are not consistent with their overall personality, immediate action is necessary. Change the direction of your approach to reestablish their interest. You have to be able to recognize and interpret the initial signs of your customer's emotions so you can correct the problem before it becomes more serious. Understand that just because a person is sometimes not forthright in their feelings does not mean that a source of discontent does not exist. Nor does it mean that they would not be open to reconciliation. However, it is often required that you initiate the aid.

THE HIDDEN MESSAGE

As stated earlier, our customer's non-verbal language is often a source of information that will provide a very accurate picture of their true thoughts and feelings. This is because people's reactionary emotions are less planned or rehearsed. However, given time to think, it is also a form of communication that you may sometimes have to decipher to understand its true message. Some are more skilled at purchasing a vehicle and have conditioned themselves to be very controlled in this situation. Sometimes your customer's emotions will be hidden or disguised. When people have time to think out and plan their reactions, their true message may be less obvious, or even a diversion. This is why you may need to search further for what your customers are truly feeling. You need to be able to recognize the inconsistencies in your customer's behavior and actively analyze their subsequent signals for any underlying motives.

People will sometimes choose to hide or alter their emotions depending on what they seek to accomplish. In some instances, your customers may seek to temper their excitement or interest to lower your expectations before negotiating. In other instances, your customers may try to hide certain feelings because they won't want to confront you with their concerns. Some customers feel it would be easier to look for the exit than continue.

As a salesperson you need to be constantly aware of the true meaning associated with the signs your customers present. These are the customers you need to be able to figure out. These are the signs you cannot afford to overlook. To be able to handle all of your customer's emotions successfully, both hidden and not, you have to set yourself up to succeed. You must become skilled in analyzing and searching out your customer's true thoughts, feelings, and emotions. You have to optimize your observation skills and then actively seek to increase your ability to understand their signals.

SELF AWARENESS

As a salesperson, you too are constantly being watched and read. Your customers are observing your own body language for the thoughts and motives you may have. They are evaluating your signals to determine qualities such as openness, honesty, and concern. Look in the mirror. How are you presented? An important part of being able to communicate effectively is being aware of the emotions you have and the way they may influence your customers. Become aware of how you look to your customers and their perceptions of you. Understand the effects that your emotions will have on others and how they may appear. Is your facial expression one of warmth? Is your body language one of openness? Is your tone of voice one of consideration? Are you aware of both your positive and negative qualities when interacting with people? Before you can grow as a salesperson, you must first recognize the strengths and weaknesses you have. Only then can you go about eliminating the negatives and increasing the positives.

FINAL NOTE

Although there are an unlimited number of emotions that you will face, the ones I have listed for you here are the ones you will come across the most. Take the time to study these emotions and possible solutions and apply them to your experiences. Understand the cause and effect of each. Develop a response ability that will aid you in understanding and reacting. Become aware of how powerful emotions are and how directly they can affect the direction of your sale. All too often, your customer may feel the easiest resolution to reclaim a level of comfort is to search elsewhere for a new salesperson, one who is able to promote a pleasant interaction and a smooth flow of the process. Do not let this happen to you. Be observant, be understanding, and be prepared. Develop the concern and instinct needed to help keep your customers headed in the right direction; the ownership of a new vehicle.

16

BUYING PERSONALITIES

Have you ever heard someone say, "We just didn't hit it off," or, "They rubbed me the wrong way?" Have you ever walked away from an uncomfortable encounter and had someone else say, "Oh, he's all right, you just have to get used to him?"

The reality is that you probably have and probably will again. So will your customers. To them, their visit is not about you, they too will walk away. The customers who enter your dealership are there to satisfy a need for themselves and will always seek to work with someone with whom they feel comfortable. Your customers will not feel the need to adapt to you. It is up to you to recognize and adjust your actions and reactions to best adapt to theirs. Please understand that customers will always naturally respond better to someone who is able to relate to them on their level. If you want to sell more cars, you will have to be able to adapt to your customer's preferred style of doing business. This includes recognizing and understanding your customer's overall presence and then establishing the best approach for each.

AWARENESS

If we are able to understand how our customers will likely react to specific actions, we will better know what to do or say in each situation. We will better know how to motivate them, influence them, and ultimately how to involve them in purchasing. The first step in improving our abilities is to become aware of the personalities we will soon meet. It is then that we can then go about better understanding their most typical actions and reactions so we are able to interact with each in an effective way.

Would you approach a shy person differently than you would an aggressive person? Would you be more likely to persuade an emotional person with information or with enthusiasm? What is the best approach when closing a defensive customer?

You are losing sales if you expect your customers to follow your own personality lead. You must recognize, understand, and adapt to theirs. This is to set the selling scene. It is to put you in the best possible position to influence your customers by increasing their acceptance of you. Different approaches work better with different people. Your awareness of this and the observation skills that you have learned will soon allow you to instinctively know your best course of action for each person and situation.

BUYING TYPES

Each of the customers we meet will usually have a guiding theme which will influence their actions and reactions in the buying process. This guiding theme is their buying personality. It is the entirety of their personal style and outward characteristics. Although there are probably more than a hundred subtle variations of "buyer types," I think most people will fall closely into only a handful. The subtle differences of each common trait and the added influence of each additional trait will still produce a somewhat defined group of buying personalities.

In the last chapter, we went over how to handle the emotions of your customers. In this chapter, we will learn how to best work with your customers in their entirety. It is here that we will seek to both recognize and adapt to their buying personalities.

Please note that as with emotions, there is no exact science in understanding someone's personality. There is only a reference created by the patterns of one's behavior. I am giving you the examples I have found to be the most common, and advice that has helped me when selling. Here again, I have tried to use the most recognized terms so that you will be better able to recognize and identify with them. However, please feel free to add to your learning by actively observing and taking note of what works best for you. My goal in this chapter is to help you gain a basic understanding of the communication and buying styles preferred by different people. It is to help become aware of your own personality and to give you some helpful advice on how best to understand others. Let's take a look.

CUSTOMER'S MAIN GUIDING FACTORS

In sales, I have found that one's outward presence consists mainly of two factors. The first and most prominent is one's level of outgoingness. The second is to what degree one is positive or not. Their measure of outgoingness will set their outward tempo, and the degree by which one is positive will set their attitude or level of amiability.

Before we go any further, take some time to picture the people you have interacted with in the past. Think about what stands out most when first meeting someone. Isn't his or her level of outgoingness most noticeable? Isn't it the factor that is most evident when meeting someone for the first time? Think of all the adjectives used to describe someones degree of outgoingness. Shy, loud, reserved, aggressive, quiet, passive, forward, pressing, timid, uninhibited, explosive, yielding, etc. Isn't it also a factor that we should be aware of when working with someone?

Similarly, wouldn't you say that one's positive or negative demeanor is the likely next candidate for describing someone? Think here of some of the commonly used descriptions: nice, mean, easy going, nasty, indifferent, cheerful, happy, dismal, pleasant, polite, rude, enjoyable, and on and on. One's positive or negative approach is a major factor in deciding the effectiveness of an encounter. Isn't this also an attribute that should be accounted for before adapting to the person attached to these descriptions?

I believe the answer to these questions is reasonably yes. I also believe that by recognizing these factors and effectively adjusting our presence to complement our customers, we will be well on our way to becoming more effective salespeople.

Our plan here is to examine the most suitable approach for each and determine how best to influence our customers receptivity to promote a positive experience. Let's now look at both the outgoing and the reserved customer and how each is influenced by our secondary factor, being positive or negative.

```
/-----------------------------------*-----------------------------------/
        NEUTRAL
        OUTGOING
        RESERVED
/-----------------------------------*-----------------------------------/
        NEUTRAL
        POSITIVE
        NEGATIVE
```

OUTGOING

Your first step in working with an outgoing customer is to determine whether they are also more positive or negative. Since they are outgoing, you will find out quickly, which is good because very different approaches work best for each.

Outgoing/positive: Outgoing/positive people are your ideal customers. They are confident, upbeat, and able to make decisions. With these people, you want to immediately present yourself in a similar fashion. Greet and present them with emotion and enthusiasm. Inspire their dreams and encourage their visualization. For these customers, it is safe to present your ideas. Although they will often have their own ideas and plans, they will be receptive to understanding yours. Seek to build your credibility early. Share and explain your beliefs on what would be their best choices and paths and then seek to initiate an action. Keep the energy high, the mood positive, and continue to move forward.

Outgoing/negative: The outgoing person who is negative is usually the most difficult to work with. Expect an abrasive person. Because they are outgoing, they will usually act on each negative feeling. If they are doubtful, they will interrogate you. If they are impatient, they will rush you. If they are unengaged, they will dismiss you. They will force their opinions, attitudes and moods on you throughout the sales interaction. They will seek and expect a confrontational experience.

The best approach here is to stay positive and friendly and keep your focus. Do not let your own emotions get involved. If you remain positive and stay away from actions that will produce negativity, you can sell these customers. Lean more to a business approach in the early stages. Keep your focus and your composure. Allow your customers to work away from their negativity with your credible information and pleasant demeanor. Let them release their energy. It is good to be confident here, but not overly assertive early on, as this may cause conflict.

Listen more than you talk with these customers. For example, stay away from statements. These customers are best influenced by your amicable questioning skills. When doing so, question slowly, allowing them to be more receptive. They will be less likely to want to argue if you refuse to argue. When you do present your ideas, present them in an open manner and allow room for their own additions. By adding their own views, they will feel that it was their idea. Their credibility is important to them. Let them take credit and roll with the decisions and plan that will take you toward the sale. Compliment them on their ideas and proceed to realize them. Note that because their nature is negative, this customer will often get a negative response. When you do not return their negative nature, they will see you as different from everyone else. If you can withstand their abuse with a smile, you will sell them a car and will probably have a new friend forever.

RESERVED

Reserved customers will be a little more difficult to understand, due to their very nature. It is here that you'll likely have to investigate whether they are also influenced by being positive or negative. Your best approach here will be to take it slow in the beginning and allow them some time to open up. It's with these customers that you will have to engage them at their own level before they'll be receptive. Ease them into a more outgoing position with your calm, amicable approach. With an approach that is too outgoing, you'll likely send these customers away. You will first have to move close enough to their style before you can attract and influence their direction. If you move in a reserved manner, you will attract them. Once you are connected, it will be easier to encourage a more open and outgoing presence.

Reserved/positive: Reserved/positive customers will often be agreeable to your ideas, but they may need some encouragement to get them to take action. My first advice here is to start the process that will increase their level of outgoingness. The key to these customers is to encourage them mildly to open up. Start with an approach that is complementary to theirs and gradually seek to increase their energy. Because these customers are also positive, they often want to open up. They are just not good at it. Small, common ground questions will work well here. Search for their interests and encourage them to share with you. Then gradually increase their level of enthusiasm with your interest in them and their activities. Try to transfer the resulting mood to your sales presentation. Just because they are slow to open up, it doesn't mean they won't. Get them started and keep them rolling. Because they are already positive, focus on their emotions. Once they are comfortable with you, they will buy from you.

Reserved/negative: Okay, here you have some work to do. These customers will not be readily receptive to your ideas or even your help. These customers are usually satisfied with their previous vehicle and are often there only to fulfill a new need. These are often customers who have done their own research and will look to you as someone who is there only to handle the details. Be cautious in your attempts to get them to open up or become more positive with an approach that is too outgoing. Your best approach here is to start slow and take one

182

step at a time. Do the best you can to accommodate their personality and assume the transition through each step. Be informative and professional. Treat them in a business-like manner. Influence them slowly to a more receptive position. If you move too fast, you will lose them. They will look for reasons to leave. Do not give them any. Inquire with questions and stay away from statements. Let them alter their own views with their own answers to your carefully structured, leading inquiries. Gradually seek to increase the impact of each question as they begin to move in your direction.

These customers are a challenge. They also create a great learning experience. Although it is always recommended to attempt to influence your customer's buying attitudes, do not feel that it's absolutely necessary to accomplish this in this case. The reserved/negative customer's decisions are usually based on need and logic. Therefore, they will not feel it necessary to have established a connection with you to buy from you. If they feel that they are in the early stages of looking, it may be difficult to promote a today purchase. However, after you create the best atmosphere you possibly can, you must still ask for the sale. Always ask for the sale. However, if it is to no avail, do not give up on future possibilities. These customers will often not allow themselves to move forward before they are absolutely ready. Set yourself in a favorable position and be sure to follow up with them respectfully, as most of your competing salespeople will not.

In the car business, you will meet many different personalities. Some will be a combination of several types. Some will be pleasant and some will be difficult. The most important thing to realize when working with a challenging personality is to never involve your own harmful emotions. Keep your feelings in check. Think of yourself as a skilled professional who responds in a manner that is only productive for the sale and for gaining you and your dealership a future customer. It is important to understand that all of your customers have different wants and desires, and will have different styles of interaction. We must learn to work with each to be successful.

A SALESPERSON'S APPROACH

Our customer's level of receptiveness is often the determining factor in our ability to sell a vehicle. Even if we have listened to and understood all of their needs, our advice will mean nothing if they are not receptive to our approach and our influence. Our goal in sales is to create the best possible selling atmosphere. One in which we can best influence and persuade our customers to make the right decision and move forward.

The most successful salesperson is one who is able to develop an outgoing and positive interaction with his or her customers, creating an optimum level of effectiveness in their sales ability and encouraging an optimum level of receptivity from our customers. Although some of our customers traits are innate and not easily altered, I believe many can be influenced with a positive and outgoing presence. If we can get our customers to open up and respond to our efforts, they will be more likely to be receptive to our persuasion and more likely to purchase. We want to be able to interact where we are knowledgeable, informative, and persuasive and where our customers are interested, receptive, and motivated; and this is best accomplished by an outgoing and positive personality. It is this temperament and disposition that will create the optimum selling atmosphere. Your obvious first step in becoming more successful is to become aware of your own presence and then seek to acquire these qualities.

KEEP YOUR PERSPECTIVE

For the newer salespeople reading this, I want to take a minute to make clear what may be a confusing objective. Please understand the reason we seek to understand and adapt to our customers is not to follow them or their lead; in fact, it is the opposite. It is to better have them follow our lead. It is to increase our ability to set and control the pace and the direction of the sale by actively aligning our personalities to complement theirs.

All too often, new salespeople will get so caught up in adapting to their customers that they will unknowingly allow their customers to take control of the sale. And, depending on their customer's intentions, the control they seek may not be leading them in the direction of purchasing from them. Seek to understand the effect of this before proceeding. Remain positive, but also remain aware of their possible underlying motives. Recognize that different customers will operate with different agendas. It is okay to love your customers, just be careful. Some people are genuine and naturally good people. However, some will need encouragement to show these qualities. This is why we adapt; this is why we seek to help them adapt.

Always look to keep the direction of your sale moving forward by adjusting and providing a comfortable atmosphere without losing sight of your sales-related plans. Our ultimate goal is for our customers to proceed through the steps of the sale with little-to-no personality resistance. Please work this out, because understanding this is very important in becoming successful. If people are comfortable in their surroundings and comfortable in working with you, they will be much more likely to move toward a purchase.

UNIQUE BUYER TYPES

The key to being able to sell to different customers is being able to recognize and understand their personalities and responding effectively to each. It is our goal to make our customers feel as comfortable and at ease as possible. Now that we have examined how to interact with the general styles of buyers, let's now take a more specific look on how to interact with some common variations.

To help get a better feel for some of the specific personality types that will come your way I am including some of the more challenging ones here. Before I do though, I would like to qualify this as well. During the buying process some people, if not most, will adopt a personality other than their usual self since the dealership may produce a higher level of anxiety than other environments. My advice is to not be offended or discouraged by any of your customer's actions. Maintain your composure and always seek to counterbalance their presence.

THE AGREEABLE AND THE NON-AGREEABLE

I started here because I think that to some extent, all customers will either be mostly agreeable or not. This is where one person will typically agree with what is said and another will typically state the other side. One will see the similarities in an item and the other will see the differences. To get an idea of the reality of this, picture yourself saying something to a customer as random as, "This is a nice truck, isn't it?"

Now think back. About half the time, the customer will respond, "Yes, it is." This would be your agreeable customer.

Another, however, will introduce the counterpoint. Since your statement was positive, a person from this group, the disagreeable type, will introduce the negative. His response might be, "Well, sure, but it's not as nice as some others I've seen," or, "It's okay, but it's not like they used to make," etc.

Where one person will agree, another will debate or argue every point you make. It is important to recognize early on which type you are dealing with, because you will need to proceed very differently with each. It's best to know how each customer will react to your actions so you can adjust your approach to receive the desired response. With agreeable customers, you want to be consultative and provide credible information. You want to present the knowledge and advice that will lead them toward a buying decision. You want to be confident and move at a good pace. Do not hesitate or look for an objection that is not there. Many salespeople will actually falter with these types of customers because they get stalled waiting for an objection that may not be coming. Non-agreeable customers however, must be handled with much greater care. Here you have to be careful not to present information that will produce a debatable response. The easiest way to do this is to present your information, and even carry on a conversation, in a question-based format. Remember, it is hard for people

186

to state the opposite to a question. For example, instead of saying, "This is a nice truck," try, "Do you think this is a nice truck?" This is true even with a leading question. For example, you could ask, "What do you like about this truck?" Since you asked what they liked, their response will be structured toward the positive.

Please recognize the importance of this. Understand that a sale has a path and a flow. Customers will not usually lead you to the sale. Sometimes it will be best to encourage a direction and sometimes it is best to discourage one. In any case, it's always important to understand how best to encourage each of your customers individually. For example, to reduce the perceived value of a certain persons trade, you may need to take a creative approach. Try, "What is it about your trade that you would improve on?" or, "What do you feel will need to be replaced next?" Lead without confrontation. Another way to persuade is by using the reverse. Lead in the opposite direction than you have planned to get the response you desire. If you have a blue Explorer that has the options they like, you might say, "I do have a blue one with similar options, but it might be too dark for you." The agreeable will accept your advice where the non-agreeable will want to see it. Learn to recognize the person you are selling.

THE EMOTIONAL

Emotional buyers will respond to your enthusiasm. They are outgoing people who'll share all their thoughts with you. They are excitable and open to new ideas. Be positive, upbeat, and agreeable. Keep your conversations personable and your presentations energized. Create a show, and they will gladly follow. Try to move along at a steady pace right into the paperwork and assume the sale.

THE UNEMOTIONAL

Unemotional buyers will move methodically. They will usually try to satisfy their needs with logical reasons. Provide these customers with information. Try to raise their level of enthusiasm by slowly bringing them along. Have patience with these customers.

Try to motivate them; however, do not get frustrated if they do not respond to your energy or enthusiasm. Understand that some people are just less emotional. Be professional, business-like, and informative. These customers do eventually buy, so make sure you follow up with them.

THE INDECISIVE

These are the customers who are not good at making up their minds. Generally, these customers want to make a decision but can't. They need and want help. Patience and gentle persistence is the recommended approach here. Most salespeople will have a hard time selling these customers because they are unable to understand what motivates them. This is because the goal may be better placed on determining what's hindering them. Search for the concerns they may have. Validate their selection with your support. Confirm that the selected vehicle will satisfy their wants and needs. Provide both the logical and emotional benefits. Reiterate that the selected vehicle was chosen based on their own criteria with their own requests. Confirm the value in your offering and then confirm that they are making a good decision. For further understanding, try to think back to a decision you had a hard time making. Put yourself in that frame of mind. Empathize with your customers and support them. These customers want to make a decision. They just need help convincing themselves. Patience and persistence are the key factors in closing these sales.

THE LOGICAL THINKER

These would be your practical buyers. These people are usually only buying to accommodate their needs. It is important to be knowledgeable and credible here. These customers will seek information for their decisions and you must be able to provide it. Pushing these customers won't result in a sale. They will have to determine all the angles in their own minds before making a decision. Your goal should be to help them sort through the information and then help point out how and why it makes sense. Help them confirm that everything adds up. Once you have confirmed this type, ease off any buying pressure and stick with the facts and information. Note that these customers are typically not interested in the fancy options and won't even seek to discuss discounts before they have made an acceptance decision on a vehicle. They will methodically move from one aspect of the sale to the next, completing each before advancing. Try to emulate their thinking when discussing how the facts line up, and satisfy their goals. Although it will be rare that you sell these customers on their first visit, with the proper investment and the right answers, you may. If not, be sure to follow up. Like unemotional customers, they do buy vehicles, just in steps, logical steps.

THE ANGRY BUYER

These customers are very demanding and usually have to get their way. To sell them, you must let them work out why they're upset. Listen and acknowledge their reasoning. Do not fear the angry customer. As long as you are able to diffuse their anger, they are buyers. Let them vent. Acknowledge that they are upset and empathize with them. Show concern. Do not try to sell them until they have released their anger. Understand that most of the time; their demeanor is a precautionary front. Kindness is your best resource here. True empathetic listening and deep understanding will open them up to you. Remember that you are a professional salesperson and don't let yourself get caught up in their hostility. Your goal is to sell a car, not fight. Be sure to control your own emotions when dealing with these customers.

THE IMPATIENT BUYER

These are the buyers that may cause you to skip your steps. For anyone new in the business, these are some of the hardest customers to work with. It's often that this customer will look to increase their level of impatience just to take and show control. Which is fine, let them, but only if they are on the path to purchasing from you. If they aren't, you will have to take control before you'll be able to sell them.

The key to selling these customers is in determining the direction of the sale, not the pace of the sale. Most of the time, their impatience is just their own state of mind. They're in a hurry because they feel they are in a hurry. If they are headed toward making a purchase, share the control with your own fast pace. You still shouldn't skip or rush your steps, just eliminate the downtime. Keep them on the move and mentally busy to help keep their receptivity high.

Although they may press you for it, do not let them rush you into giving them a discounted price without building value or without a commitment. You will lose these customers faster than most if you give price information too fast. Confirm their commitment before the negotiation. If they are just there for information, take control and slow them down. This customer will generally give you the time as long as they feel you aren't wasting it. A skilled salesperson will be able to present the value stage and still keep them engaged. When you do get a commitment, proceed with the sale. These customers will buy. They just don't want to be bothered with the little things. Close the deal and let them know you'll handle all the details. Assure them that you will make certain everything is handled properly.

THE ARROGANT BUYER

These are the customers with big egos. With the right approach, they will be your easiest sales. The first step is to position yourself as one of the top salespeople. Act with strength and confidence. These customers do not want to work with the average. They want to work with the best. Their opinion of themselves requires this. Let them know of your sales awards or recognized achievements.

Once you have positioned yourself to be on their level, try an approach that will both feed and challenge their ego at the same time. Listen to their stories and admire their power. Let them be the center of your attention. Create a show just for them. Give them the experience they are looking for and then ask them to buy. If you set this up right, they probably will make a forward move and purchase. They will not want to seem indecisive or unable to buy. Your confidence will pay off here. The key is to recognize these customers early and not react negatively or confront them. Your goal is to sell a car and not get caught up in an emotional battle. Think of yourself as a technician. Respond appropriately to their actions without involving your own emotions.

THE SHOPPER

These are the customers who want to stop at every store in town and compare prices. The only way to sell these customers is to slow them down. If you give them a discounted figure before you have an established commitment to buy, you will have a very short future with them because they'll leave for the next dealer. It is here that you need to have the willpower to succeed. Your resolve to build the necessary value in yourself and your dealership will be tested against their resolve to get a price and leave. It is that simple. If you give in to their demands, you'll have lost any chance of making a sale. This style of customer may also appear within many other personalities. You will have to adapt to their overall personality while still taking the best steps to sell them a vehicle. Keep your personality attuned to theirs, but keep your resolve as well. These customers are usually very skilled at making you believe that the only way to sell them is by giving them a price. However, trust your process. Do not allow them to intimidate or influence you. No exceptions. Never, ever offer discounted figures on the phone or in person before you have taken the time to create a bond, built the appropriate value, and received a concrete commitment to do business.

FINAL NOTE

Many customers have come to expect a lack of compatibility with salespeople and will often set up excuses upon their arrival. One of the most popular is, "I'm just looking."

Well, yes, they are just looking. Unless of course they happen to find a salesperson that they feel is open, receptive, and capable of handling their needs, someone they feel is pleasant to deal with and complementary to their style.

The people you meet will often be willing to work with you; however, they will unlikely feel the need to adapt to you. Think of some of your own experiences when shopping. Have you ever come up with an excuse to leave because you didn't feel comfortable with the person you were with? Understand that selling cars is not like selling cheeseburgers or fries. People know they are going to have to spend some time with you. Most will only want to proceed with a transaction that they feel will be pleasant and favorable. Most customers will not tell you that they are uncomfortable with you. They will not want a confrontation. Most of the time, these customers will just humor you with some questions and ask for a card and a brochure. However, could this result be different if the customers were truly engaged by the salesperson's effectiveness in complementing their personalities? The answer is yes. People will want to interact with you and will want to purchase from you if they find comfort and compatibility in working with you. Believe this and success will be yours.

17

TRAITS OF A TOP SALESPERSON

Character traits are something we all have. They are the habits we have formed over time that guide us in everything we seek to accomplish. They are the patterns we have developed that shape both the way we express ourselves and the way we interact in the world. Our set of traits is our unconscious guide. They have an impact on everything we do, including the results we are able to produce.

Certain habits are helpful to being a successful salesperson, and certain habits are not. For example, picture the difference in production of someone who is proactive versus someone who is inactive. Picture the objection handling ability of someone who is persistent versus someone who is easily dissuaded. It is easy to understand that the person with the better habits or traits will sell more cars.

Now take a minute to picture your own traits and the effect they may have in your sales efforts. Understand the influence that each has to offer. Analyze your current presence and determine the traits you need to keep, add, or adjust. To be successful as salespeople, we have to align ourselves with the proper traits and look to eliminate or diminish the traits that may be holding us back. We must understand the power of our traits and how they influence our ability to produce.

Developing the proper character traits takes the same two ingredients involved in reading this book; desire and initiative. For example, you have the desire to become a better salesperson, so you took the initiative to read this book. To redefine your character and achieve success in sales, you have to be able to search for and attain these factors. You must identify and examine the traits and habits you have and then adjust them so you can succeed. You must understand the strength of their influence and then develop your own strength to amend them. Your traits and habits were not formed overnight, and it may take considerable energy to develop new ones. However, if it is truly your desire to achieve higher results, search for the initiative. Find the strength within yourself and take control of your own success. If you have the initiative and strength to get started, time and momentum will aid you in your goal. Your positive traits will only become stronger and more dominant. Take the initiative to get started and take the initiative to succeed.

OUR TRAITS DEFINED

Here are some of the traits, habits, and philosophies that successful salespeople share. Let's take a look.

MOTIVATED

The number one trait of a top salesperson comes from within. It is the desire to succeed. While we all have some measure of desire, only those able to define and utilize theirs will become the best in their field. To help develop your own personal motivation, you must first realize what inspires you to want to succeed. Only then can you go about working on how to best achieve your success.

The sales profession is a business for performers. It offers the freedom and opportunity to achieve any level of success we want. If you have chosen sales as a career, there is likely something within you that makes you want to succeed. To further establish your driving factors choose what you most want to accomplish and use it to aid in your motivation.

What are the factors in your life that will further encourage your success? What is it that you want out of life and your career? Is it status? Is it money? Is it security? Do you owe it to your family to be successful? Analyze and separate what makes you move. Think

194

about what drives you. If competition is a motivation of yours, track previous sales results and strive to surpass them. If money is a motivation of yours, reach for that next bonus level.

Once you realize your individual motivations, position yourself to be influenced by them. Allow them to influence your production in a positive way by keeping them present and active in your mind. This will help you set yourself up for success and will also take the work out of selling. It will keep you active in enacting your skill, not just in performing a task. Please know that the people who excel in their fields are the ones who are motivated to succeed, not the ones who feel they are just working a job.

GOAL DRIVEN

A goal is an accomplishment you wish to attain. It is something that is desired and set to encourage your motivation. It's the prize you will enjoy if and when you accomplish what you set out. Whether you are new to the sales business or just looking to restart your career, you can increase your motivation by setting yourself up with some specific goals.

When setting your goals, take the time to think about the things you want. Imagine some of the items and rewards. A goal can only be effective if it is something you truly desire. Once you set your goals, build on the framework to achieve them. Position your goals to influence your actions. Soon the achievement itself will become part of your reward.

Goals should be meant to challenge you, to push you further than you would normally go. Your goal is the achievement; your motivation is attaining the reward you have tied to it. To get your motivation started, set the goals that will encourage your actions and reward you in the near future. Enjoy your rewards and use them as motivation for your next goal. Then start to mix your reachable short-term goals with some long-term goals to keep yourself motivated and build for your future. Build one step at a time. An example long-term goal in the car business would be to create your own customers. To achieve this goal, become your own business and do your own marketing. Stay in contact with your previous customers and ask for referrals. Do not let your success be based on how many people come in the door or current market conditions. Having goals such as this will help keep your focus and ensure future success. Use the mix of your goals as a basis for a long term pattern of success.

Determine and set your goals. If you take pride in having sales as your profession and look at it as your future, take the time now to set some goals. You will not be able to completely release your energy or reach your potential without first understanding your motivations and establishing your goals.

PROACTIVE

This is one trait that all successful salespeople will have in common. It's the ability to harness the power of their motivation and take action. It is the ability to act and react when an opportunity arises. This trait, when combined with persistence, is the difference between succeeding and failing.

When you see an opportunity; move forward. Learn what it takes to be a top salesperson and then develop the skills needed to become one. Successful salespeople are opportunity focused. Take charge and control of your actions. Do not let your goals and dreams pass you by. Take the initiative to prepare yourself to succeed, and then take the initiative to succeed. Create your path and take it. Start with the principles and steps in this book. Learn the proper selling skills, develop your people skills, and put yourself in motion. Do not fear your mistakes. Use them to learn and grow. Once you are in motion, you will always be able to change and adjust your actions to better succeed.

CREDIBILE

Credibility is the key to being persuasive. You have to be able to present yourself as a credible salesperson before you will ever be able to influence your customers. If your customers do not feel you are capable of helping them reach a decision by providing the proper information, they will not be open to the influence needed to sell them a vehicle.

Credibility in sales requires two elements. First, you have to show an understanding of your customer's needs. This is accomplished by asking the proper discovery questions and listening to their answers. They have to believe that you understand their needs before they will feel you are capable of helping them. Secondly, you must be able to give accurate advice regarding their needs. This is where your product knowledge comes into play. Know your vehicle line and know how their benefits will relate to your customer's needs and wants. Position yourself as an expert. Know and believe in the benefits of your vehicles. You must be able to portray your belief in yourself and your product line before you can ever expect your customers to believe in you or be influenced by your advice. Understand that credibility can only be gained by inquiring about and understanding your customer's motivations and goals before you start to present your inventory. A top salesperson will establish his credibility by asking the proper questions and solidify his credibility by providing the proper guidance.

PERSISTENT

Selling is a series of steps in which you may find resistance to proceed in each. Successful selling is having the persistence to amicably overcome any resistance and proceed with the sale. Being successful is similar to finding a solution to a problem. Being persistent is having the drive to find the answer. Salespeople who are willing to try different solutions and refuse to give up will sell the most cars. Having the persistence to solve your customer's needs, concerns, and hesitations will often lead you to the sale.

There is a philosophy in the car business that it takes an average of five attempts to close a sale. I believe this to be accurate. However, without persistence, we would never know.

Do not deny yourself the benefit of persistence by not wanting to feel too forward. Persistence and being too forward, otherwise known as pushy, are not the same. Let me explain. Being too forward is asking your customer to make a move without giving them new information. Being persistent is creatively searching for a solution and then asking them to make a new decision based on the new information you have provided. Understand that your customers are there for a reason and may just want to be persuaded. Develop the will and perseverance to continue your efforts and always help them achieve what they came for, a nice, new, shiny vehicle.

CURIOUS

Curiosity is having the desire to understand what it takes to make a sale. It is what will drive the top salesperson to question and search for the answer to each obstacle presented. Discovering the proper information in sales is crucial to gaining insight on how best to proceed. In sales, a successful questioning process is the key to success, and curiosity is its driving factor.

I think we all have some level of curiosity; some of us just need to develop theirs a little further. Start by asking why and why not. When you are in a selling situation and you face an obstacle in moving forward, make sure there are no unanswered questions. Leave no stone unturned in finding your direction. Have the desire to understand why things are the way they are. Do not accept resistance or failure without trying to understand what happened and why it happened. Make a commitment to yourself to understand what will motivate and persuade your customers to move forward. When you know why or why not, you may have the right answer. Without knowing why, you will not know why. Got it? Ok then, use your curiosity and persistence to search for the answers.

VISUALIZING

With your imagination and creativity, you have the opportunity to visualize the sale ahead of time. Visualization is a powerful tool in the sales process. It will help you prepare your path and recognize the obstacles you may encounter before they occur. The actual sales process will become more fluid because it will be a re-creation of your visualization. This will give you the ability to act and react better in each situation.

Before your appointments arrive, try to picture the process and direction you will take throughout the sale. Imagine your greeting and how you'll build rapport. Think of the questions you will use to identify your customer's needs and imagine the various responses they may have. Play the different scenarios over and over in your head until you can feel them. This will give you the opportunity of a practice run and will ultimately enable you to feel more comfortable and better prepared for the real thing. This is a form of rehearsing for the future, kind of like practice makes perfect. Isn't it easier to do something a second or third time as opposed to the first? Try this, and you will instantly see the results.

DRESSED FOR SUCCESS

As the saying goes, first impressions are everything. Take the time and effort to increase the quality and credibility of your clothes. Look the part. Dress professionally. Salespeople who are professionally dressed are more influential with their customers. This is your first available offering of credibility.

Think of some of the people you see for services in your life. If your plumber showed up wearing a suit and tie, you would question his ability to handle the service you asked him to accomplish. It is the same in sales. You have to look the part to be accepted as credible and able. As a salesperson, you should try to look successful without overdoing it. If you are selling Acura's or Audi's, a suit and tie may be recommended. If you're selling commercial Ford trucks, a clean pair of slacks and a pressed company shirt would be a suitable choice.

POSITIVE PRESENCE

Have you ever heard the expression, "They have a magnetic personality"? Try to picture the person they were talking about. It may be an actor, a politician, the leader of a country, or the salesman next to you. Their natures are such that anyone can identify with them. Well, examine what they have that enables them to be so liked and accepted. Is it their smile, their charm, their character? Study the compassion they have and share with other people. Recognize the traits in them that you can adapt to yourself. Learn to create a level of evenness and consistency when interacting with your customers. Work and interact in a way that is comfortable for them. Be a person of the people. Picture yourself and your service as acceptable and welcoming to all. Creating the proper presence will always help your ability to be persuasive.

PROPERLY INFLUENCED

In the automobile business there are many different qualities of salespeople. To be a top salesperson, it is important to emulate the other top salespeople, not the underperformers. Whereas one will help you, the other will drag you down. Watch and learn the habits of the best achievers. How do they greet people? How do they carry themselves? What is their presentation style? What are the questions they ask? Take note of the success of each and analyze their actions. How does each manage his or her time? How do successful salespeople get their prospects? Understand that different people will have different levels of success for a reason. Search out these reasons and examine the qualities that may aid in your success.

EMPATHY AND COMPASSION

Empathy is involvement. It is being so close to your customer's presence that you can actually feel what they are feeling. It isn't just recognizing someone's feelings. It is a deep form of understanding. When they are mad, you are mad for them. When they are happy, you are happy. You feel their pain and you feel their excitement. You share their emotions as if they were your own. Understand that the car business will often produce an atmosphere of anxiety, and the better you are at diffusing this anxiety, the more cars you will sell. There is no greater bond or feeling than trust as a result of someone willing to make an emotional investment in someone else's needs.

EMOTIONALLY IN CHECK

Like it or not, people are judged more by the emotions they project than by the feelings they may have. How people are perceived is greatly influenced by the reactions to the emotions they are experiencing. In sales, it is important to diminish the signs of your negative emotions and be more open and expressive with your positive emotions. To present a more positive, outgoing presence, you must understand your projection and learn to control the reactions that your various emotions may exhibit. Understand it is the disposition of your emotions that you will be judged upon, not what you are thinking. It is how you appear that will be seen.

Although you may not have a choice in whether to feel an emotion, your reactions can be chosen. This is something you can alter with the proper awareness and conditioning. Learn to accept your emotions, but control your reactions. Believe that a positive presence will have a positive impact and a negative presence will have an adverse effect. In a sales interaction, is it more important that you are happy or that you project that you are happy? How you portray yourself is ultimately what will decide the effect you have on other people. Don't you agree? Even the most successful salespeople have the same emotions and capacities as others; however, they have learned to keep their emotions in check. Become aware and adjust your actions to form a more open and positive image.

FEARLESS

Do not let fear limit your success. Understand that fear is the reason most people don't accomplish their goals. It may be fear of rejection, fear of failure, or even fear of the unknown that will stop you from reaching your potential. Fear may stop you from asking for the close and making the sale. Fear may also limit your persistence. You may be the most courteous and knowledgeable salesperson around, but if you do not have the courage to ask for the sale, your efforts will be wasted. Seek to recognize and conquer your fears. The best cure for fear is knowledge. Know that it is your knowledge that will give you the confidence you need to perform at a high level. If you learn your product, learn your process, and learn how best to work with your individual customers, your level of fear will always be surpassed by the natural confidence inspired by your knowledge.

A thought technique that may help you move past certain fears is to examine the worst-case scenario. Picture the worst result that could happen as a result of your action and then think of your response. If you rehearse positive responses, you will feel more confident to proceed. Another thought technique is for you to understand your best potential for gain. Realize if you do not try for something, you

202

won't likely achieve it and this will equal not having tried at all. So, if you think about it, you really have nothing to lose, do you?

FINAL NOTE

There is such a slight skill difference in being able to sell five cars a month and twenty cars a month. But it happens every month. In the same time period, one salesperson will talk to the same number of people and invest the same amount of energy, and yet the disparity in their results will remain constant. One will consistently outsell the other. In auto sales, a deal is measured in inches. It is the little things that are imperceptible to most that make the difference.

For those of you who've been in the business for even a little while, I have a question. Have you ever looked at the twenty-plus-cara-month salespeople and wondered how they do it? What is it they're doing? Well, I'll tell you. It is attaining the qualities and traits such as these. It's being able to create a unique connection with their customers that exceeds the circumstance of their meeting. Do not doubt the effect of these traits. Accept the need and seek the change to align yourself with the proper traits.

18

QUESTIONS ANSWERED

Sales takes a lot of self-acceptance and pride to be successful. It is essential to have a clear mind and be at peace with yourself and your profession in order to perform at your best. Whether your customers are consciously aware of it or not, they can sense your level of credibility and confidence. This is the same credibility and confidence that is needed to influence and persuade your customers to make a purchase. To have this sense of self-belief, you must be free of doubt and have a clear focus.

I want to take the time here to clear up some of the questions you may have regarding your own perception of the sales profession. Here are some of the biggest questions I have heard from beginning salespeople, and some advice regarding those questions.

SALES IS AN HONEST PROFESSION

The whole business world revolves around the salesperson. Without sales, there would be no business at all. Without salespeople, no one would ever be able to enjoy any of the wonderful products that are available.

Have you ever asked yourself how you can be comfortable being a salesperson with all of the less-than-positive references people make? Well, my answer is simple. Be proud of yourself and be proud of your profession. Being a good salesperson does not compromise your principles. In fact, all truly successful salespeople rank high in honesty, integrity, and compassion. Refuse to let anyone think the profession of sales is a dishonest one. The goal of a successful salesperson is to bring a solution and enjoyment into their customer's lives by helping them get what they want and need. Learn to care for you customers and you will soon have plenty of them in your future.

SINCERITY

Many new or unsuccessful salespeople have a difficult time understanding their values and principles and the roles they play within our business. For many, it is not just how our business is sometimes viewed from the outside, it is also their internal set of morals or conscious that they may question.

Many salespeople will ask themselves, "How can I be sincere when my goal is to sell a car?" The answer to this is simple as well. The more sincere you are, the more cars you will sell. The more needs you understand, the more solutions you will provide. If your goal is to push someone into a car that you know does not suit them, you will fail in this career. People are perceptive and will sense your intention. The lack of trust you portray will limit your ability to persuade. You can only expect to truly build a productive career if you establish yourself as a person with a solid character. Before you can succeed in any field, you first have to set yourself up to succeed. Understand that the person who wants to understand people and their needs will sell the most cars. Write, rewrite, or enhance your own sense of values. Become the person it takes to be successful, and you will soon be well on your way.

INCOME

Money is an important factor in the world. It is a product that will often be attained and thought of in many positive and possibly not so positive manners, justifiably or not. As a result, many of you will ask: How can I justify making a profit when our goal is supposed to be to help people?

Well, okay, this is a good question, so let's reason this out. Think of yourself as a problem solver, someone who seeks a solution for the needs of other people. You are providing a service. You are a professional. You have studied your vehicles and practiced your skills. If you are able to help your customers with a solution, do you deserve to be compensated?

If you're able to assess their goals and use your knowledge and understanding to help find the vehicle that is right for them, should your time and effort be rewarded? The answer is yes. Selling cars is a business, and there are costs and incomes associated with running a business. Think of other professionals who provide a service. Would you expect a doctor, a lawyer, an agent, or an accountant to accurately solve and complete your needs for free? When they handle your task, are they in some way compensated? Yes, they are, and you should be too.

Any successful company in the world is probably that way for a reason. In our business, and in most businesses, there is a high level of competition. We are in an open market. Staying profitable and staying in business takes both quality production and sensible pricing. If good companies gave away all of their products or services, there wouldn't be any good companies left in business. In the business world, isn't it the companies that perform the best that are also the most successful? Additionally, shouldn't you, if you perform well, be compensated well?

The key to becoming and remaining a successful salesperson is to provide a quality experience and a successful solution and yet be profitable for you and your dealership. This way, you and your dealership can be there for your customers when they need service and are looking for their next car. All successful businesses have created a balance of quality service and fair compensation, and car sales should be no different. A salesperson's profit should always be equal to the level of service they provide and the performance they achieve. The more solutions you provide and the better you are at performing your service, the more successful you deserve to become. All successful salespeople are and should be dedicated to providing their service well and dedicated to being well compensated.

REJECTION

How do you deal with rejection? Well, there's no way around it, rejection is a part of this profession. It is safe to say that not everyone will want all of your cars all of the time. However, even knowing this, salespeople will still sometimes feel the negative impact of being rejected and often ask themselves how they'll ever overcome their feelings. Well, the answer to this is not so simple. The answer to this is something you must look at and analyze from within and from different perspectives. It is something that you will constantly face and must condition yourself to both understand and overcome.

In the sales profession, there are generally two levels of rejection you will come across. There are the small rejections you will continually face during the sales process, and then there are the more permanent rejections that occur when unable to complete a sale. Let's look at each.

For the first instance, understand that during the sales process, you will often be confronted with a show of resistance from your customers. In this case, know that this rejection is often reactionary and only temporary. It is impossible for your customers to agree with everything that occurs or is asked of them all of the time. Learn to accept this and proceed only in the manner that is best. Do not let their resistance inhibit your ability to proceed. With this level of rejection, know that your persistence, creativity, credibility, and knowledge are the keys to your solutions. Understand that you will have these temporary rejections and prepare yourself for them. Understand their occurrence and follow your process to overcome them.

Now in the second instance, you may incur a more definitive level of rejection. When you are unable to complete a sale, your sense of rejection may be a little more difficult to shake. Here, you will need to look within yourself and concentrate on the positives. You will need to stop, refocus, and start again. You will need to understand your own internal determination and refocus your confidence and self-belief. Do not allow yourself to get down on yourself or your career. Understand that sales is a continual learning experience, and there is no better way to learn than when facing adversity. Learn to look at this rejection as temporary and only as a learning experience. Be happy in knowing you will most likely face your next interaction more knowledgeable and better able to handle the objections.

When dealing with rejection, take solace in knowing that you will never truly learn what not to do until you fail, and failing is always only temporary as long as you keep your willingness to learn. It is only when you no longer feel the need to learn that you will set yourself up to fail. Search and understand what happened and learn from it. Know that with every new customer comes a new start. Please believe that if you keep moving forward and retain each experience as a lesson, you will always succeed in the long run.

SALES DOWNTURN

Sales slumps will occur. Why? Well, there is no easy answer to this question. However, they do occur and will at various times and for various lengths. A sales slump is a period of time when little or no sales occur. The reason for this may be, and usually is, a combination of a cyclical happening and a negative outlook from within ourselves. As we said earlier, confidence and self-belief is important in sales, and the lack of this may perpetuate a slide. Make sense? Well, just to make sure, let's take a further look and start at the beginning.

To help ease the possibility of getting uninspired, try to understand that sales are just sometimes strong or weak at certain times. Sometimes it rains more often than not. We do not know why. Have you ever noticed at certain times there is no one in the store and at other times you're packed full? Why is this? Did everyone get together and time their visit? Not likely. In some cases, it may just be the cycles that occur at various times in people's lives. Sometimes it just works that way. Now, if you expand this time period to a typical week or month, you will see the potential for slow periods in longer circumstances as well.

In addition to this "fate", there will also be more rational reasons as well. Other, more probable explanations, such as large public events, economical swings, seasonal changes, and even the timely influence of local and national news may enhance or affect certain patterns of traffic.

These reasons, along with the negative impact of a lack of momentum, may in fact produce a period of slowness. However, know that this reasoning, explainable or not, shouldn't be an excuse for you not to be determined or optimistic about your future. Always know that with your hard work and efforts, and your persistence to succeed, you will always eventually break through any slump and continue to higher grounds. Stay prepared and remain focused on your future. I am only bringing these possible explanations up so that the salespeople who are dedicated and persistent will be less likely to allow any temporary slowness to affect their motivation or future goals. Use this philosophy to not let yourself get discouraged, however at the same time, continue to implement the many ways to help lighten any future sales slumps. Make use of your slow times to help create your future success and limit your exposure to these downturns. Take this time to focus on your prospecting. Prepare for your future by actively seeking to develop your own customers. This will keep you occupied and less likely to be affected by any temporary downturn, explainable or not. Understand there will always be factors that are not in your control; however, there will also always be factors that are in your control. Learn to take control of the factors that are and you will be less likely to be guided by the factors that are not.

Sales is not a sit-back-and-wait event. Sales is a continual process of production and preparing for production. If production is low, prepare for a more productive tomorrow by being active today. Oh, and remember: slump or no slump, with one sale, you're right back in the game.

FINAL NOTE

There will always be the potential for uncertainties to occur in our profession. Sales is a profession that will constantly be subjected to outside factors and influences. You will often be challenged by the questions that present themselves. However, know that most of these questions can be resolved if you take the time to work them through. Your desire and resolve will give you the strength and answers to succeed. Look at each question as it applies to you, and search for the understanding that works best for you. Resolve your questions and overcome your obstacles. Do not allow yourself to be influenced by anything or anyone. Develop your sense of peace and stay determined to maintain it throughout your career.

19

THE TELEPHONE

The telephone has a purpose in the auto business, and it is a definitive one. The purpose of the telephone is to arrange a convenient time for you and your customers to meet at your dealership. It is for you to set an appointment.

There is a reason that there is an appointment board in every dealership. It is because that is how you sell cars. It is also where you sell cars. You should not try to negotiate a deal over the phone. Your only motive when calling or answering the phone should be to get your party to come in and visit you and your vehicles in person.

The first step in becoming better at bringing people in is to realize and believe that what the salesperson says will matter more than the specifics of what your dealership has to offer. Some salespeople are consistently successful at getting people to come in, and some are not. So it would only stand to reason that it is the salesman's ability that will decide if a customer makes a visit, more so than what the dealership has to offer. There are too many other special deals and vehicle choices available to be able to consistently bring your customers in on the value of your offerings alone.

Your customer's desire to learn more and make a visit is best created by developing both their rapport and their curiosity. If you have not sufficiently created a rapport with your customers, they will have no common interest on which to base a visit. Additionally, if you offer all of the details of your sale or inventory up front, they will lack the curiosity needed to visit. They won't need to come in, they will have all the information they need to make a comparison elsewhere. They will likely then call the next place to see if there is a better deal there, and you can believe there always will be. However, by creating a bond and balancing the supply of answers they give, skilled salespeople can be engaging and still leave their customer's curiosity intact; the same curiosity needed to increase their desire to find out more and encourage a visit.

UNDERSTAND THE CALL

The most important factor in understanding the call is to realize the intent of your calling customers. It is to recognize and trust that the sole reason for a customer's call is to decide if they will visit or not. It is for them to determine if your offerings warrant further research. This is why, to be most effective, you must understand that your sole effort should only be to increase their desire to visit. It should not be to provide callers with too much information or attempt to accomplish too much in trying to complete a sale. You must first have your customers agree to visit before you can get them to agree to buy, and this is always best accomplished by increasing their curiosity, not by satisfying it.

CONTROL AND RAPPORT: ALWAYS THE BEST PATH

The most important factor in consistently being able to set an appointment is for you, the salesperson, to establish the structure of the call. It is to set and influence the overall mood and direction of the conversation by following the process we will soon lay out. It's to take the lead of the call by initiating what questions are asked and to what measure their questions are answered, all while being proactive in increasing your caller's agreeability and receptivity in feeling both interested and desirous to learn more.

The best way to establish the structure of a conversation is to be the one that initiates the questions, and the best way to keep it is by promptly following each of our questions up with another. Because our customers will likely open their conversations with a question, we must look to exchange our position. Simply answer your customers question and then, without pause, follow your answer up with a question of your own. Answer then ask. If ignored and asked another, answer again, lightly of course, and politely ask again. As you establish your direction with the questions you ask, you can then start to look for the transitional questions that will help lead you into asking for the appointment.

MAINTAIN THEIR WILLINGNESS

Being effective on the phone is directly dependent on the amiability of your individual customer. Your ability to be successful necessitates a balance. You want to stick to your objectives and accomplish all you can, but you also want to acquire their agreement and receptiveness by adjusting your approach. Taking the lead in a sales setting is always best accomplished with skill and finesse.

If your customers are aggressive, seek to calm them. If your customers are tentative, seek to relax them. Your best approach is to be courteous and professional. Understand that there will be some possibility of contention in your phone conversations. The exchange of information may not always flow smoothly. If your customers are direct and insistent on having their inquiries addressed first, you may have to answer their question lightly and deliver a level of satisfaction before attempting to find the information you want. Think of a ballet, not combat, when trying to receive the information you want. Keep a balance between the information you request and their willingness to give. Sometimes if you keep pushing, they will keep backing up. However, if you ease off and back up when necessary, it's often easier to get them to move forward.

KEEP YOUR PROCESS

The key to getting better at bringing your customers in is to seek to adjust your approach, not your process. Know that the mood of any conversation can always be pleasant, even while you seek the completion of your goals, because the nature of any conversation is more determined by how something is said than by the specifics of what is said. You may sometimes have to do more or less adapting or rapport building, depending on your customers demeanor; however, you still always want to maintain your goals.

THE TELEPHONE PROCESS

We are best able to create an interest and increase the odds of having our customers visit by having a set process and following it every time. This process is a step-by-step path designed to lead customers to the appointment.

- Answer with enthusiasm

- Answer initial question lightly

- Get a name and number

- Create a bond

- Further curiosity

- Set the appointment

- Confirm the appointment

- Reconfirm the appointment

This is all there is to it. Do not overcomplicate it or let yourself get off track. Keep it simple. Don't let potential customers run you all over the lot in search of minor details. This will only limit the possibility of them visiting. Simply let your customers know that all of their specific questions will be answered upon arrival. Establish the completion of each step and then move on to the next.

EACH GOAL EXPLAINED

ANSWER WITH ENTHUSIASM

People want to communicate with people who are bright, cheerful and pleasant, and do not want to communicate with those who are not. Your first goal is to answer the phone right. Clear your mind and turn it on. Eliminate your distractions. Answer politely and professionally, and most importantly, with some enthusiasm.

Understand that your manner and expression can and will set the entire tone of your conversation. Greet them with a smile, give them a chance to identify why they are calling, and set your path. A large part of your ability in selling will rely on having the proper phone skills. These skills start here. Focus all of your attention on the person you are speaking with and start to create the desire for them to visit.

THEIR NAME AND NUMBER

Okay, get their name and number. No problem, you might say. I'll just ask. Well, not so fast, it's not always that easy. In fact, any experienced salesperson will tell you that there may be a lot more involved here. Many customers will often not be forthcoming with their information. In fact, a salesperson will often have to plan for receiving this information and should always take the steps to ensure he or she is in the best position to obtain it. When it comes to getting a customer's name and number, there are three things we should understand. They are: why we want this information, why our customers may not want to give it to us, and most importantly, how to get it. Let's look at each.

WHY WE WANT THEIR NAME AND NUMBER

Obtaining a customer's information is our first objective when answering the phone. As a salesperson, you always want a way to follow up with any potential customer. If for some reason an appointment cannot be set after the first conversation, it makes sense to have a way to get back in touch with them, right? Additionally, there may be times you do not have access to the facts that will help create their interest. At other times, you may not be at your best and may need another opportunity to initiate a visit.

Another reason to get your customer's name is so you can use it in your conversation. Remember, people wake up and respond when they hear their own name. Also, if you have their name and number, they will be less likely to skip the appointment or not ask for you at arrival. Your customers will be more likely to come in and visit you if you have the information needed to re-contact them and reconfirm their interest if needed.

WHY CALLERS MAY NOT WANT TO OFFER
THEIR NAME AND NUMBER

However, many customers may be hesitant in giving their information. The customer you are speaking with may have had a bad experience in the past. They may have had an inexperienced salesperson re-contact them too often, and will guard against this happening again. In fact, many customers will prepare for this and have become very good at guarding their information.

For example, you may ask, "Sir, can I have your name and number?" He might respond with the following: "Umm, I'm at work," or, I'm in transit. I'm hard to get a hold of. I can't be reached. I can't take incoming calls. I don't want anyone to know I'm looking at purchasing a vehicle. I'm leaving town later tonight. I don't have a phone, etc., etc. And who can blame him? No one likes to deal with an inexperienced, pushy salesman. However, you need this information, so you have to separate yourself from the average and become skilled in both getting this information and handling it properly when you do get it. Let's take a look.

HOW BEST TO GET A CALLER'S NAME AND NUMBER

Our best chance of getting our customer's name and number is to obtain them before we satisfy their quest for information. Understand if you give too much information early on, they will be much less likely to give you their information later in the conversation. We will then be at their mercy to contact us, and they probably won't. Although you may be tempted to start with the information they seek, you must restrain yourself. People will generally be willing to give something if they want something. However, if they already have what they want, they won't feel the need to give up anything. They may no longer feel they need your service and will not want to be contacted. So, first things first.

When trying to get your caller's name and number, think of the laws of human nature. The first law here is give to get. Many people are naturally instilled with a sense of fair play. Although a person may resist making the first move, she or he will almost always be willing to follow your lead. Here's the plan.

Right before you ask your customer for their name, give them yours. It is human nature for people to return the favor, "Hi, my name is JB, and yours is?" Most people will offer you theirs just to be on even ground. They will feel the need to balance the flow of information. These are habits that have formed with the help of society, peer pressure, and even schooling. This form of balance is considered playing fair.

If they ignore your inquiry and continue with a question, simply try again after they finish. As we spoke of earlier, answer their question lightly and repeat the question you desire. An example response for this might be, "Okay, let me get that information for you. My name is

JB, and your name is…?" or, "Yes, ma'am, I believe that offer is still available, let me double check that. My name is JB, and yours is…?"

When you are finished, just pause and wait for a response. From here, if your customers are not responding, just keep repeating this step, nice and calm. Give a brief answer and reattempt for their name. Just be sure to keep the conversation friendly and flowing. In some cases, you may have to take a break with some rapport-building conversation and maybe even offer additional indirect information before you reattempt. The key here is to remain calm and amicable without getting frustrated. Trust that this works, and with a little real life practice, it will soon be easy for you.

This step can be repeated for the caller's phone number as well, "John, do you have a pen? Okay, let me give you my 800 number. It is…" Then, with no pause at all, continue with, "And your best number is?" or, "John, my most reachable number is…, and yours is…?" Give information to get information. Remember that in sales, you constantly have to play to the laws of human nature.

Another hint to get a caller's phone number is to get them started by giving them what you think is their area code. For example, you could start out by saying, "Great, let me get that information for you, and your most reachable number is 410…" Then pause. It will be a natural reaction for them to finish it for you or correct you with the proper area code and continue with the number. Again, people cannot usually take the silence you have left. They will need to speak. They will not be likely to leave an empty or incorrect blank out there. They also won't be likely to ignore your request and upset you before they have the information they want. Even if they had decided before the call that they would not give out their number, this will usually encourage an easy response.

If these attempts do not work, it is probably safe to say that they are guarding their information. However, after we have built more rapport or lightened the tone, we want to try again. An additional attempt can be to appeal to their sense of past experiences. How many times have you been disconnected when being transferred or put on hold? Use this to your advantage. When your customers ask you a question in the course of your conversation, offer to put them on hold while you are, "checking on that for them." When you do, just say, "Okay, and your number, in case we get disconnected, is 410...?" They will almost always give it to you at this point. If they don't, let them know that it may take a while and you do not want to risk not being able to help them. Portray that it is your goal and your job to get them the information they need and for this you will need their number, just in case.

If their evasiveness continues, and they are still reluctant to give you their number, it is probably time to acknowledge their obvious concern and assure them that you will respect their information and not overcall them. Let them know you understand their reluctance because you, too, have been in this position. Put yourself on common ground. Let them know that you also dislike pushy salespeople. Then reiterate that your only goal is to help them get the information they have requested and you want to be able to return their call if new information should arise.

NOTE

An important note to bring up here is that once you have a caller's return information, you want to continue your phone process and ask for the appointment while you are still on this first contact. Many salespeople were taught to get their customer's numbers by offering to get their requested information and then calling back. Well, if this is the path you have chosen, once you have their information, don't look to hang up and call them back. Always continue trying to set the appointment. Do not take the chance of them cooling off or getting busy with something else. They may call someone else right away and set an appointment with them. So, even if your intention is to call right back, it may be too late. Encourage a visit and make an appointment without disconnecting your current connection. Get their name, get their number, and continue for the appointment while on your first call.

MAKE A FRIEND

The next step in our process is to build a rapport. There is nothing better to ease the flow of communication than a friendly relationship. Much like when you first meet someone in person, search for common ground and build upon it. When conversing, practice slipping in some common ground questions with your discovery questions. Try to find a connection between you and your customers. Search for the people, places, or things that will create your bond, your relationship. It is surprising the common ground you will find when you start to search. Your common ground search can almost be played like a game. How many degrees of separation are between you and them?

Maybe you went to the same high school or maybe your aunt once visited the same vacation spot. Start general and focus in once you sense a match. A good opening may be to ask where they are calling from and take it from there. As your rapport develops, adjust your approach. The best way to accomplish a rapport is to allow them to open up with their likes. Let them take the lead you provide. Enable them and then let them go where they want. The opening common ground you reveal will allow them to be included in the rapport. It will allow them to open up and relate to you so that they will feel more comfortable. Always allow the main focus of the conversation to be interesting to them.

When you learn their wants, you will know how to fulfill their needs. When you develop rapport, they will want you to fulfill their needs. Your callers will be much more likely to come in if you can create a bond with them. If they like you, they will look for reasons to do business with you. Once you have established a friendly

222

connection, do you think that they would rather come in and see you, or call the stranger who happens to be listed next in the phone book?

ADJUST YOUR APPROACH

In some cases, when seeking an appointment, you not may need a rapport, and in all cases, you should not force someone to develop one. If a caller appears focused on coming in anyway and their tone is purely business, allow an appointment based solely on that. For example, if they open the conversation with, "Hey, I'm about to head over there, and I wanted to make sure that this listed vehicle is still there," your phone rapport is unlikely to be necessary. Initiating too much side conversation in some situations may be seen as insincere or wasteful to your customer's time. Always seek to quickly get a feel for your customer's buying personality and adjust your approach. If you can be seen like your customer, in this case, professional yet all business, they will more than likely reciprocate your businesslike response and ask for you. For this step in the phone process, it is all about being able to read each situation effectively and adapting. Just be sure to have your customers write down your name and number, in case they get lost or are running late, and be sure to get theirs as well.

KEEP THE FOCUS ON THEM

To your customers, their call is about them, not about you. Keep the focus on them and their benefit in coming to visit. Additionally, when trying to set an appointment, do not say things like, "Please visit me. I need the sale," or, "Come in and help me with my month."

Present and display the benefit to them, not you. Their impending purchase is for them and their wants, not yours. They did not call with the intention of giving someone a sale; they called to find a solution for themselves. Only when you have an established rapport and shared concern for each other can you bring yourself in as a factor for them purchasing based upon your benefit. Keep your conversation positive, friendly, and flowing, and always maintain the focus on how their visit will benefit them.

DEVELOP THEIR CURIOSITY

Now that we have their return information and have started a rapport, it is time to determine our customers interest and further develop it to entice a visit. It is time to increase their curiosity. Your goal here is to give your customers enough information to have them want to come in, but not so much that they won't need to. You want to build on their interest with selective information but not satisfy it by leaving no question unanswered. Do not just randomly present all the knowledge you have on a particular vehicle or on the details of the sale you're having. Seek to answer their initial inquiries, and then lead into your first attempt for the appointment. Let's look at an example.

If your customers open their contact by inquiring about a specific vehicle or deal, your response may be, "Yes, I believe that vehicle is still available, we also have many vehicles with similar options. When would be a good time for you to come in and see them all?" Very little pause here. "Would it be convenient for you to come now or would this evening be better for you?"

This sequence of questions is one you should learn and learn well. It answers their question and still increases their curiosity. It also forces them to answer a question of yours, one that will derail their second question which was likely another information-related question. As stated earlier, this is where you need to take and maintain control in the conversation. Note also that the option you give at the end of your response makes it easier for them to answer. When they answer, simply follow up with your next question that will either lead you into your rapport building or your quest for their name and number. Again, your best direction here is to follow the process.

Also, stay away from specifics like individual stock numbers or small features as you proceed with your conversation. Even if you have a similar vehicle with better features at a better value, you will often have a hard time convincing them of this on the phone. Seek to do this in person. Both you and your customers have a job here. It's their job to receive the information they want and decide if they will visit, and it is your job to have them visit so you can afford them the opportunity of investigating all your dealership has to offer. It is your job to position yourself to make a sale and position them to fully consider all of their opportunities by having them visit.

Understand it is not your job, as a salesperson, to strictly be a source of information. Let your customers know that the various vehicles you have all have different features, setups, and purchasing options, all of which you would be happy to go over with them in detail in person. Being a little vague is okay here, otherwise, you may be limiting their opportunities by having them not come in.

Additionally, never allow your customers to state too many of their goals in the course of their communication. Even though you won't have to specifically address their goals at that moment, many will still hold you accountable for not offering the fact that their goals didn't lineup when they do visit. I am reviewing this because quite often, this is something customers will attempt. Many will want to state exactly what they want and then inquire, "Do you have this available?" Many will feel that this is the easiest way to inquire and determine if a trip is necessary. However, if you let them continue and build their perfect car or deal, it will be very difficult for you to say, "Come in because we can offer exactly that." Your goal should be to stop them, mid-sentence if necessary, and reiterate that you have many available offerings. "When is a good time for you to come in and see them all?"

WHY WE LIMIT

Since limiting our information is such a large part of our appointment-setting process, let's take a little time to understand why. Offering too much information is likely the leading reason that most salespeople are not able to set the appointment.

I think it is safe to start by saying that all motivation to visit is likely either accomplished or not accomplished by the information communicated. If we are firm in our resolve to persuade them to come in for the most vital information, they will be more likely to come in and open themselves up to more options and possibly a better decision. You have to believe this. You have to be strong and trust this.

Understand that curiosity in itself is enticing. People wonder about the unknown. People do not want to be left out. Their desire to solve their curiosity is what gives us the leverage to have them visit. Take this leverage and use it; do not throw it away by satisfying all their requests. When they inquire about a specific vehicle, answer with a question like the one listed above that will lead you to the appointment. If that question doesn't work right away, reword the question and try again.

If their question is so specific that it requires a yes or no answer, find another variable with additional inquiries, "Yes, ma'am, that offer is available until the end of the month, would you be interested in looking into our finance offer as well? Yes? Okay, great. My name is JB, and yours is...? And in case you are running late or get lost on the way, let me give you my direct line. And your number is...?"

If she says no, know we still have other questions. Try: "Okay, well, let me ask you a question, are you flexible on your choice of colors and options or would you prefer to come in shortly, while the selection is still good? Have you seen our latest color; the new shade of Autumn Red? Is anyone else involved in choosing the various options? Have they seen all of the available options?" etc., etc. As you can see, there is a never ending supply of questions that can both intrigue their curiosity and encourage their motivation. When you sense their curiosity has increased, ask for the appointment!

ESPECIALLY THE PRICE CALLER

Keeping the curiosity high is especially advised for the "what's your best price" caller. If you give this caller a specific discounted price on a specific vehicle, you can believe they are likely never to come in or call back. They will use that price as a basis for their next phone call.

Always look for a variable that is part of the equation, but has a varying value and is hard to determine on the phone. This could be their trade or a non-specific option on one of your other choices. Indicate they might be missing out by not investigating all of the variables in the sale in addition to all of the other options of other vehicles and programs. Let them know that many times in the past, when someone has come in with pre-set plans, they soon altered their plans upon discovering one of your other available options. Ask them, "You wouldn't want to settle on a car without investigating other choices and decisions, would you?" Have confidence and approval for the vehicles you represent. Be excited to convince your callers to come in and take a look.

For the extra tough "price" customer, be persistent in letting them know that you have lots of similar vehicles at similar prices, however, your first concern is finding the one that is right for them. Do not become unsettled and run to your manager for pricing every time someone wants to know the lowest price. Assure them that you'll be extremely aggressive on price, but for their own best interest, you want to make sure they are happy with the specific vehicle before they make a yes or no decision based strictly on price. Let them know that it would be pointless to negotiate on a specific vehicle now if they choose another one when they arrive. Alert them that you feel compelled, as a conscientious salesperson, to make sure they will be happy both before and after they spend their money. You want to make sure the vehicle they ultimately choose is right for them before they get caught up in a price negotiation.

This should make sense to them because it does make sense. Make them feel as though they will be losing out if they don't come in to see what you have to offer before allowing themselves a decision based solely on price. This is worth repeating. I understand that it's often difficult not to give your customers all the information all the time, but again, you have to be strong and do what's best to make a sale, not what your customers say is best. Conserve your information to help entice a visit. It is this caller's goal to get all the information they can from you and then use it as leverage to get a better deal at another dealer. Do not, I repeat, do not let this happen to you. Search for a motive other than price and build upon it. It might be you, the dealership, your service department, or even the city where your dealership is located. Whatever it is, find it. Do you want to be a name and a number on a piece of paper as they walk into another dealer, or do you want to be that dealer? Trust that setting an appointment is best accomplished by offering selected pieces of information and creating the promise of more when they visit.

SET THE APPOINTMENT

When it is accepted that they will visit, set the appointment for a definite time. "Later in the week," is not an appointment likely to be kept. Try to narrow it down by giving callers an alternate choice of times. Encourage them to choose one time or another. This will help you get the process started while still allowing them to choose the time. This way it's easy for them to choose, and because they ultimately do choose, it kind of becomes their appointment. And of course, they will be less likely to break their own appointment, right?

For example, you may ask, "When would be a good time for you to come in?" Slight pause. "Would it be convenient for you to come now or would this evening be better for you? Great. Is it better for you around seven p.m. or would eight be easier? Great, I'll see you then." Lead people to narrow-in on the choices you give them. This is the best way to set an appointment, so it will be our only way.

When they do give you an appointment, simply confirm the appointment. Do not go back to the information stage. That's like still selling after they say yes. Remember, you do not want to risk satisfying their curiosity. Get the appointment and confirm the appointment.

CONFIRM THE APPOINTMENT

After you have set the appointment, it's time to confirm the appointment. Reiterate the day and time they have chosen, so they will hear it again and further note it. Give them the impression that you take your appointments seriously, "Okay, Mary, it was nice talking to you, and again, we will see you at seven o'clock on Tuesday."

Ask for the appointment, confirm the appointment, and reconfirm the appointment.

RECONFIRM THE APPOINTMENT

Sometimes the conversation may not always end exactly when you think it will. Some other small instance may come up. Every time one does, always re-end the conversation with the confirmation of the day and time of the appointment, "Okay, Mary, great, and again, we will see you Tuesday at seven o'clock."

FAILED TO SHOW, NOW WHAT?

If your customers scheduled time has come and they have not shown, call and ask if they are running late, this may reinitiate them to visit if they had decided to not show. If they answer and say that they are unable to make it, say you understand and set another appointment.

However, if you are unable to get a hold of them, here is a plan to help have them visit in the future. Call later and apologize for missing their appointment. Apologize almost to the point of embarrassment. Make sure you include an excuse or possible reason why you were unable to be there for them. When you convince them of your regret, offer to make it up to them by meeting them at their convenience. Then offer to make their visit, "extra worth their while," to increase the value.

At this point, they will probably feel bad for you taking all the blame and look to make their next appointment. They will also want to avoid the feeling that you displayed. They will often declare that they understand and be eager to set another appointment to relieve their own guilt. This allows your customers to save face and not feel as if they would be scolded by you if they did still want to come in. If they are still in the market, this almost always works. Try it. The more you apologize, the worse they will feel, and the more likely it is they will show.

CREATING OUR PHONE SUCCESS

Earlier, in the chapter *Traits of a Top Salesperson*, we talked about how our traits and habits so definitively decide what we are able to accomplish. We talked about how we are sometimes limited by our current traits and how we are able to increase our ability with the addition of new, more positive traits. We also talked about how difficult some habits are to alter. Well, I think that this is never more evident than when looking at our habits concerning the phone. I know from my own experience in selling and in training that taking the lead in our phone communication is very difficult to accomplish completely and effectively. Few people will become fluid on the phone overnight.

It often takes a lot of focus and conditioning to be able to do what you are supposed to do, let alone do it well.

I think part of the reason for keeping our obstructive phone habits is that the average calling customer is constantly challenging our phone process. Since it's the purpose of our callers to seek information, it is often our impulsive reaction to answer. It is human nature to want harmony. You have likely formed your habits around what you feel is pleasing to the people you are speaking, and the easiest way to accomplish this is to respond in a manner that satisfies their wants. An example of how common it is for salespeople to simply be a source of information, and how conditioned some have allowed themselves to be, can be found in this frequent conversation ending question, "And is there anything else I can do for you?" Well, you can believe that when a salesperson asks this question, there will usually be no visit; all of their inquiries were satisfied. It is human nature to seek fulfillment, and the shortest path to receive it is always the easiest. However, to be successful, we have to do what is right to best to sell a car. We have to set our focus, effectively take and keep control of our phone interactions, and only look to set the appointment. We have to condition ourselves to follow our process, stay away from completely satisfying our customers curiosities and still keep our harmony. Always believe if you are skilled and practiced, you can still keep your customers amiable even while you position yourself for a visit.

FINAL NOTE

Making an appointment, like closing, is similar to solving a problem. It is having the creativity to decipher the best way to increase your chances your customers will visit your store. The key to making an appointment is influencing your customer to want to make an appointment, not just asking them to make an appointment. It is being enthusiastic, friendly, inventive, and persistent. Understand and have them understand that without visiting you, they will not have the opportunity to explore all of the opportunities available to them. I understand that you may sometimes succeed in attaining an appointment by doing nothing more than being a source of information. Yes, it may happen that all of your information has lined up perfectly: no rapport, no curiosity, no name, no number, and no confirmation of the appointment; just the facts and you got an appointment. This scenario is possible. However, the odds are not in your favor. This will not be your best chance for a visit. For consistently positive sales results, you should always position yourself for the best possibility for a sale to occur. Listen to your customers and understand their motivations. Then proceed to build on their motivations to create the curiosity and the desire needed to visit.

20

LISTENING

Sales is not just jumping in and telling your prospects why they should buy. Sales is first listening to your customers and understanding their goals before you start to speak. It is a two-way interaction that will engage your customers with both listening and understanding.

Your ability to communicate effectively is one of the most important skills in sales, and listening is its foundation. It is how we are best able to understand our customers and how we show we are capable of helping them. When our customers see our desire to fully understand them before we go about our presentations, they will feel comfortable with providing us additional and accurate information. This is the information we need to have before we can help influence a purchase. This is the same information they will feel we need before they allow us to influence a purchase.

AWARENESS

Were you ever unable to make a sale and couldn't understand why? Were you ever just left standing there all alone and confused? Well, I ask you, was it possible that you missed what your customers were trying to say? Did you effectively enable them with the opportunity speak?

As I said in the introduction, there is a fine line between making a sale and not making a sale. In many cases, a sale is going to be a challenge. To be consistently successful, you have to take and use every advantage available to further your chances when working with your customers.

Proper listening skills are essential. We must become aware of this before we can ever expect to excel. Although this will certainly be a short chapter, I do not believe that this should be considered not crucial in making a sale. I really feel you should try to realize how much your ability to make a sale is affected by your ability to listen before determining your next best move.

HOW TO LISTEN

To help with our listening ability, let's take a look at the process of listening. Recognize and understand the relevance of each step. Allow yourself to become comfortable in listening by consistently following this pattern until it becomes second nature. And, although listening is listed as a process here, please know it is not supposed to be seen as such within your interaction. Listening should always appear as just a natural flow of communication.

THE LISTENING PROCESS

- Clear your mind of your own thoughts or feelings when starting to listen.

- Place yourself to receive what they are saying.

- Encourage them to speak openly and candidly with your own show of openness.

- Face your customers to best receive what they are saying.

- Become interested in what they have to say.

- Adapt your position or stature to theirs as you begin to learn their style.

- Do not let other salespeople, your surroundings, or other interruptions distract you or them.

- Ask the questions and provide the responses that will further your customer's flow of information and provide you with additional details on their wants and needs.

- Acknowledge what the customer is saying. Don't argue or finish their sentences for them.

- Listen with all of your senses. Focus on the customer's feelings as much as their words.

- Observe their body language and voice inflections to verify the true feeling of their words.

- Develop an understanding of their goals and parameters.

- Confirm what they are saying by repeating their main points.

- Save determining your response and next action until they have finished with their point.

- Recognize and understand what your next action should be before you reply or react.

LISTEN FOR YOUR PATH

In some steps of the process, listening may actually be harder for many salespeople than talking. The reasoning behind this is that many salespeople are often enthusiastic about the vehicles they have to offer. They know their offerings and are desirous to present them. However, they will often present what they feel is important with their own wants or needs in mind and will focus on their own specific routine. This routine will often sound canned and not intended for their specific customers. It is here that these customers will feel that their salesperson doesn't understand or care about what is best for them. They will feel that their salesperson did not even listen to them. Do not place yourself in this position. A successful salesperson will always present the features and benefits their customers deem important. They will listen to their customer's wants and needs and cater a presentation just for them.

CREATE THE ENVIRONMENT

Please know that customers will not always walk up and volunteer everything needed to find a solution. It is you that must often provide the environment for them to be forthcoming. Sometimes you will enable your customers to speak simply with your open manner. However, sometimes you will best encourage them with your inquiries.

The actual skill of listening is only part of the complete process of listening. Your ability to listen is often only possible if you are able to create an experience that allows a communication with your customers. Listening is often the response that is only enabled by the questions you ask. In addition to increasing your ability to listen, be sure to increase your opportunity to listen. Understand the benefits of asking the proper questions. Understand that effectively inviting your customers to speak is always the best first step in understanding what they are trying to say.

INCREASE YOUR ABILITY

Earlier in the book, when we talked about understanding people from our observations, our listening skills played an important part in our ability to understand. Listening is more than just hearing what your customers are trying to say. It is absorbing the whole projection of how and what they are saying. It is listening for your customer's true feelings and intentions. It's examining what was said, why it was said, and even what was not said, within your conversations.

The easiest way to understand the benefits of listening is simply to spend more time listening than speaking. The next time you are involved in an interaction, pay attention and seek to understand what your customers have to say. Become aware of how your communication is perceived and analyze its ability to help you act upon the information necessary to achieve a sale. Change your approach, if necessary. Temper your desire to just talk your way into a sale. Listening and understanding is the best plan for almost every step in the sales process. You listen in order to best know how to greet, build rapport, select, present, negotiate, overcome objections, and close. Listening is how you start each step.

EMPATHETIC LISTENING

Empathetic listening is the deepest form of listening. It is feeling the way your customers are feeling by placing yourself within their emotions. It's putting yourself in their position and looking out from their point of view. Empathetic listening is important for when your customers are confused, upset, angry, or concerned. It will help resolve or lighten your customer's present emotions in order for them to best move away from their current thoughts. It is also helpful when your customers are hesitant in moving forward. It will allow you to feel as they feel. Understand that varying needs will often require varying intensities of listening.

Empathetic listening involves an open mind. It is not waiting for your customer to finish so you can respond. It is not prescribing a remedy before they are through. It isn't selective listening in which you pretend to see their point of view. It is clearing your mind and focusing on truly understanding. Before you can accurately seek to help your customers, you must first understand what they are thinking and feeling. Empathetic listening will put you on their level and better allow you to receive the information that will help diffuse and resolve each situation. It will soften your customer's focus on what is distracting them and better allow them to think about purchasing an automobile. Empathetic listening may involve slightly more time and patience, but it is an investment well spent. It will save time in selecting a vehicle, presenting it, and persuading a move forward. It will also greatly lessen the possibility of losing the sale due to misunderstandings. Empathetic listening will help you determine the best path to take when your customers are preoccupied with concerns.

ALWAYS LISTEN, YET KNOW WHEN TO FOLLOW

Due to the varying motives and shopping abilities of the customers you will face, I wanted to include a section that will help prepare you to understand why it is so important to listen and analyze before you act.

When enacting your listening process, listening to understand means just that; it means to understand. It does not mean listen to follow or carryout whatever your customers say or ask of you at each step of the sale. This is an important fact that you must understand. For example, depending on the stage of the process you are working in or the context of your customer's requests, you may or may not be best advised to follow through and complete all that is asked.

The information you receive while listening to understand is to help lead them. It is not for them to lead you. Listening to understand is for the purpose of understanding your next best action and continuing your customer's forward direction. You should always listen to what your customers are saying, however, there will always be situations in which you should first evaluate and then calculate your response to fit each situation. To listen effectively, you want to take the customer's specific information, combine it with the knowledge and skill you already have, and then formulate the best path to help them discover and realize their next best move so you can lead them to a purchase. Once you have successfully helped select their vehicle, you want to set the direction of the sale. It is you who is best advised to

238

understand and listen to your own direction before you respond. Let's look at some examples of this reasoning.

- When a customer says they want a vehicle that will accommodate four people and also be able to haul small loads of landscaping supplies, you should listen and try to accomplish what they have asked while helping to select a vehicle.

- When a customer asks you to give them your best price on a particular vehicle so they can compare it to the next dealer's price, you should listen to their intentions and plan your approach to alter them.

- When a customer says they want their monthly payment to be less than a certain amount, you should listen, but you can't always assume that they will not be willing to pay more if the vehicle that they really want necessitates that they do.

In each situation, there is always a unique best response. Always understand your objective and path.

LISTEN BETWEEN THE LINES

By now, you have probably heard the advice to "read between the lines." Well, this is also how we should listen. What, where, when, and how someone will tell us something is all information that we can use to better understand what our customer is actually saying. Most of the time, when communicating, our customers will be pretty straightforward in what they say and we, as professional and successful salespeople, should be pretty straightforward in how we listen and answer. After all, we want to understand our customers goals and offer our best effort in helping them achieve their goals. We also want to be sure to continue to make their future ownership experience a pleasant one by providing a high level of service after they have purchased by listening to and handling any concerns that may arise. However, you must still remain aware that in certain cases and at random stages in the process, our customer's words may not always be best received at face value.

When responding or reacting, you always want to take the best path and this may or may not advise you to follow their lead. A common example of this can be seen in the preparing-to-negotiate stage. Here, certain customers may choose to enact methods that may be less than forthcoming to benefit their own position.

In the day-to-day interactions you encounter, there will always be occasions that necessitate your own determination of what is best for the sale before you act. These examples are just some of them. Your best path depends on the motives and agendas of your specific customer at the time. Listen to understand, not to reactively follow.

Remain conscious of the motives your customers may have and react accordingly. You must be prepared to interpret their words in order to understand each circumstance.

The best way to prepare yourself to move forward is by effectively listening to your customers with the intent to uncover all that is said and expressed. It is to listen between the lines. It is to listen to understand. It is to apply your listening process, through both verbal and physical measures, to open yourself up to completely identify with all that is being communicated. The good news here is that in some context, directly or indirectly, most customers will tell us exactly how to sell them a vehicle; we just have to be able to interpret the information they offer.

FINAL THOUGHT

In a perfect sales world, all of our customers will come in and say exactly what they want in a new vehicle, will want to purchase right away, and will be completely flexible when determining the purchasing terms and conditions. In reality, however, it is rarely that simple. Because of this, you will often have to prepare for the obstacles your customers will present while proceeding through the process. You will have to learn the best paths to take and then trust in these paths enough to follow through with each.

Learn the process and then trust the process. Listen to your customers goals and then construct the best path to achieve them. Recognize their wants, concerns, and intentions before you act. Follow the process of listening, learn, and understand. The best way to sell a car is to do what is best to sell a car. If you listen with all of your senses for the true meaning of your customer's words and actions before you determine your best next move, you will absolutely sell more cars. Listening to understand is the smart way to communicate and is a sure step forward in becoming a more successful salesperson.

21

PROSPECTING

Prospecting is the act of developing your own customers. To be a top salesperson, you must not limit yourself to the people walking in the door. You have to set yourself up to create your own business. The key to successful prospecting is to be proactive. You have to take the initiative to develop a way to build up your customer base so that you will always have a steady supply of prospects.

Before you actively go out and seek new customers, you should first set up a system to interact with them. Start by developing a method to organize the lists of your potential future customers. From here, you can add to and develop these lists to proactively pursue their business and the business of their friends, neighbors, coworkers, and associates.

CONSTRUCT A DATABASE

For a small investment, you can purchase mailing list software that can easily be installed on any computer. Basically, this is a modern day Rolodex, but one that is easier to use and does much more. This is the simply the easiest way to have an available list of your customers, and it will enable you to contact them at will. Once it is installed, opening your database will be as easy as clicking on the icon on your screen. Once open, it will appear as a column graph sheet, where you can simply add the name, address, and phone number of the prospect to the list. The extra columns provided within each list give you the ability to add other information, such as the make and model of the vehicle sold or the sale date. This will let you create focused mailings for the unique events you choose, defined by the criteria that you select.

CREATE YOUR LISTS

Now that you have created a database, you can start to develop the groups of people you would like to keep in contact with. Start out with a list of your friends and relatives. Then add a list of your neighbors or people in your community groups. Of course, as you start to sell, make a list of your customers. Just take a few minutes every other day or once a week to add your new sales. This is very easy to do, and once they're added, they are there for your use at any time.

If you look at the most successful salespeople in your dealership, most will have a method they use to regularly contact their customers. That is how they got to be successful. Every salesperson has potential prospects. The salesperson that contacts and stays in touch with those prospects will also have customers. Please take a second to understand the relevance of preparing for your future. If you spend all your time waiting at the front door, your production will always mirror current market conditions. During the slow periods, you will not have the traffic available to continue selling at a high level. It is wise business to take time to develop future business. If a paper company spent all of its time and resources gathering trees without planting new ones, it would eventually run out of trees. For a short while, the company's production would be high, but it would limit its production capacity in the future. Being successful in the present, as well as in the future, lies in the balance. Selling automobiles is much like running a business. Start to develop your business and future now.

KEEP IN TOUCH

Once you have some prospects in your database, you can easily print envelopes or postcards for all of them in one sitting. All you have to do is click on the data entry screen and enter the number or folder of the prospects you want to mail. The printer will take the card one by one and print the name and address of your chosen prospects. Or you can have a mailing company do it for you. When you assemble your prospects using different criteria, you can create the selective mailings you choose. For example, you could mail your friends and neighbors an invite for an event, or mail your recent customers a thank you.

The more you are in contact with your people the more they will think of you when they or their friends are thinking of a new car. Be creative and create the types of letters or cards you like and include small messages that fit your selling style. I have always liked postcards because they are fast and relatively inexpensive. Also, most everyone will look at a postcard because there is little work involved and it usually fits into their attention span. Your local printer can print you up a postcard with just about anything you want on it for pennies apiece. You can then add your targeted recipient using your mailing list software. Use your creativity in the message you put on each card. You could have your postcards preprinted on the front and handwrite a message on the back if you want to portray a more personal touch.

Of course, they probably use a Rolodex, but how do you think the veteran salespeople in your dealership have so many people coming in and asking for them? They keep in touch with their customers.

DEALERSHIP LIST

Another source for future customers is your own company. Most dealerships have been open for a while and have many previous customers. As with most stores, salespeople will come and go. This will leave many orphan customers. These people will most likely be your store's future customers because they already have a history with your store. There is already a big start here on the rapport and comfort level. Be proactive and ask your manager for a list of these previous customers. Then just enter them into one of your folders and treat them as your own. These are your inherited customers. This list is like gold.

It still confuses me how few salespeople think to ask for orphan customers. If you can get a list of customers who bought there three or four years ago, you will be in customer heaven. Many will ask for you right away upon receiving an inviting contact from you, and many more will come in after a few mailings. With very little work and expense you can postcard hundreds of people a month. In your first greeting, start out with a small introduction. Let your new customers know that you will be there for them for all of their dealership needs. It is probably best to start out more as a customer service representative. Then let your own personality and creativity take over. This is very effective with your neighbors and previous customers as well, as many will send you referrals. Not everyone will come in at once, but over time, many people will come in asking for you. And let me tell you, when they do, they are almost a guaranteed sale. This will help keep your momentum up and create a good addition to the people coming in through the door.

When mailing, include your name, phone number, and some sort of incentive to visit. Be creative. Develop your name as your brand and come up with your own personal message as your trademark. With the messages you send and proper repetition, you can effectively create a positive perception of the service you seek to provide.

BUSINESS LISTS

There are many different business groups you can prospect. Look in the phone book for local auto repair shops. This is a great source of people who may be looking for a new vehicle. Introduce yourself to the owner or manager and let him know what you do. Build rapport over time. You could add each business to one of your mail lists and keep in contact with them on a regular basis. These shops will know before anyone when their customers are, or should be, in the market for a new or newer car.

246

One of the best businesses to visit and obtain contacts from is your own service department. Get up early one morning and introduce yourself. In this surrounding, customers will probably know what you're doing, so be upfront. You might say, "Hello, my name is JB, and I was curious when you might have an interest in a new car?" Ask them when, not if. You will get a more specific answer. They might just smile and take your card, but note if their bill is more than expected, they might just give you a call. Ask if it would be okay to get their information so you can keep them informed about any specials or upcoming promotions that may arise. Seek their names and addresses and add them to your list. Offer to be their contact for any of their dealership needs. If your dealership sells trucks or vans, you could target service-related companies. Once you develop an in with these companies, you will have a strong source for repeat business.

Insurance companies are another good source of potential future customers. Whenever I sell a car, I add the insurance agent to my mailing list. I start with a small letter, letting them know I helped one of their clients purchase a vehicle and that I will be there for them if they need help or if they know of anyone else who might be in the market for a new vehicle. Prospecting is the start of business relationships.

CARRY YOUR SIGN WITH YOU

Carry your business cards with you wherever you go. Whenever you do business outside the dealership, let people know what you do. Everybody knows somebody who is or might be in the market for a better car. Also, when you go out in the world, let people know that you like selling cars. People always prefer to do business with people who like their business.

FINAL NOTE

Prospecting is more than just advertisement. It is a continual form of branding. It is choosing a message and strategically placing it for your audience to see. It is developing how your intended group of prospects will think of you simply by seeing the image or message you have chosen. All big companies have a logo or catchphrase; you should, too. It can be your name or even just the fact that you keep in contact. Try to come up with some common factor for them to easily identify your mailings. Remember, what you are really offering is your service. What you are really selling is you. The more people see "you," the more familiar and comfortable they will become with you. Prospecting is a continual process, one that grows and gets stronger with time. Do not get discouraged in the beginning and give up too soon. Think of prospecting as adding a little something extra for now and building for your future. Once you get started, it takes very little energy to keep it growing. Invest in your future. People will always prefer to do business with someone they know or someone they have had contact with recently. So contact them. Market yourself. When you are able to attract and keep your own customers, you will have truly reached self-employment. You will be responsible for your own destiny and well on your way to being a top salesperson.

22

THE INTERNET

The internet is much like the phone in that it is an opportunity to set an appointment. In relation to our business, it is a marketing tool, much as radio or print. It is a method for our companies to attract an interest and an avenue to obtain an inquiring prospects contact information. It is a lead management system that will supply and organize our responding customers information and provide us with an easy-to-use way to start our communication. For our purpose as salespeople, it is simply a resourceful method to encourage a visit.

HOW THE LEAD SYSTEM WORKS

Most dealerships have some form of a web-based system that provides a platform to allow access to the internet driven leads directed to your company. This is a website hosted tool that will format your company's web-based communication into an easy-to-use management system. Meaning, all of the leads that come in from the various websites that your offerings appear on, will be directed to this one dedicated site. This is an easy way for your company to allow you access. Once received, you can start the process of having potential customers further their involvement by encouraging their visit.

UNDERSTAND YOUR MARKETING

Most of the websites that your dealership will use in its marketing efforts seek to engage the researching customer. This is accomplished by providing a way to make an offer, a way to request additional information, or simply to offer a response if customers supply their name and contact information. The most likely reason that your customers have used the internet to contact your store is because they were searching for information and the website that they were on requested them to inquire.

The reason to understand your marketing is to understand how best to encourage your customer's desires. Become aware of what they responded to in order to better understand their motives and goals. Visit your sites to get a feel for what is being offered, as well as how it is offered, so you can better understand how your customers are driven to respond. It is up to your management team to decide how and where they use the internet to market your vehicles, but understanding these marketing ideas can be extremely helpful when interacting with your new customers.

SET THE APPOINTMENT

Our main objective in this stage, as with the phone inquiries we will receive, should be to set an appointment. We will not be able to sell a vehicle over the internet, just as we will not be able to sell one over the phone. Our potential customers will still have to come in, select and drive the vehicle of their liking, and proceed through the steps of purchasing a car. In some circumstances, such as businesses or buying services in which customers are internally restricted to competitive bid prices only, an agreement may take place. However, for the vast majority of the leads that we receive, we should treat them no differently than we would an incoming call. Please believe and understand that the public is simply using the internet as a point of preliminary contact. This contact is no different and should be treated no differently than contact on the phone. Similar to the phone, the best way to work or interact with our provided leads is to keep the focus on setting an appointment. Seek to set an appointment.

RESPONDING TO INQUIRIES

Okay, now that we have a basic understanding, let's take a look at how best to engage our customers and then some advice on how to get our communication started.

ENCOURAGE THEIR INTEREST

The first step when responding to your customer's inquiries is to open a line of communication. Engage them. Create a response that will encourage people to respond.

Before responding, read and attempt to understand the customer's goals in contacting you, and explore all of their provided information. Look for the motivating factor in their inquiry and create a question that will entice a response. You always want to respond as fast as you can. If a phone number is offered, call them. If none is, then email them right away. Determine their goals and then develop a preliminary strategy to set an appointment.

I know that some schools of thought are that you should provide all the information requested, including price, as fast as possible. However as a general rule, I disagree. Your objective here is to set an appointment, not to be a free source of information and price provider. I firmly believe that the best way to have your customers respond is to entice them with partial information and a question of your own. Our goal in responding is to provide enough information to keep our inquiring customers sense of accomplishment high enough to feel satisfied to continue and yet limit certain information enough to have them still want to seek more. Then, using the customer's desire for more, create an interest and feeling of potential worth so they will want to further their quest with a visit. You want to encourage a response with your questions and further their interest by way of curiosity. Using their inquiry as a way to sense their key interests, seek to respond with a question that will encourage them to want to answer. Find your customers key interests and use them to open the lines of communication. Supply both comfort and a compelling desire at the same time. Got it? I really hope this make sense, because understanding, believing, and trusting in this is essential in performing at your best.

ALWAYS KEEP YOUR FOCUS

To some, this advice may seem obvious and overstated, however, many unsuccessful salespeople still seem to have a hard time grasping and following through with this reasoning. I have seen firsthand where this never seemed to settle in with some of the less successful.

Many salespeople will simply issue a response to their customers with some included information, then sit back and hope the customers will somehow appreciate their information so much that they won't seek further advice or additional sources and will come in and buy without being asked. They will also hope that the customer will not want to compare or research their information elsewhere. In addition, these salespeople must further hope that all of their provided information lines up perfectly with all of their customer's parameters. These struggling salespeople have somehow convinced themselves that by being a great source of information, they will be rewarded. They believe that their job is simply to provide answers and then wait for their customers to offer a meeting.

A successful salesperson, however, knows that this is not often the case. A successful salesperson knows that this offer and hope method does not usually fare well. As stated in the phone chapter, information alone will rarely manufacture a desire to visit. Conversely, it will quite often manufacture a desire to seek additional guidance from another member of the profession at another dealership.

252

ENGAGE YOUR CUSTOMER

BY WAY OF PHONE

When your customer provides a phone number, use that as your first point of contact. It is always easier and timelier to try to set an appointment over the phone. You want to take the most direct approach when first seeking contact. Remember, your customer may have also made another inquiry elsewhere, so time is important. When calling, you will either get your customer's voicemail or reach them in person. In either case, your first goal is to entice them to respond with interest. Let's take a more detailed look at both, voice-mail first.

VOICEMAIL

When you reach your customer's voicemail, your initial goal is simply to have them want to respond. It is to have them follow your lead. The best way to accomplish your goal is to leave a message that they will want to respond to. When leaving a message, always entice the customer to respond. A good message to leave would be to lightly answer their initial request and follow up with a question of your own or a promise to provide additional information upon their return call. Following our theme, the easiest way to do this is with the promise of more or new information when they call back. Do not answer all of their inquiries on the machine. It is your customer's goal to seek information to decide whether to make a visit. It's not yet for the purpose of buying, so one step at a time.

An example may be, "Hi, this is JB from ABC motors. Yes, I believe that vehicle does have a sunroof. When would be a good time to go over some of the lease offers you inquired about?" or, "Hi, this is JB from ABC motors. I have some information on the available lease program. How long were you thinking of leasing? Give me a call at... this afternoon, if you could."

253

Notice that you can vary your response depending on where you feel the emphasis of their motivation is. When they call back, simply seek to set an appointment so they can visually see and drive their interest and you can further explain the additional incentives available. The key to selling a vehicle is to remember the steps and keep your focus. Entice a response, entice a visit. Keep in mind that you will only be able to sell them something when they are in your presence, not over the phone.

Another similar message to leave, again, depending on the directness of the customer's question and your feeling of their intent to respond, may be even more vague and also possibly more enticing. Here, you would just leave your contact information along with some general information before finishing up with a promise to deliver new information when they call back. An example here may be, "Hi, this is JB from ABC motors. I wanted to let you know that we have many similar vehicles in stock; in fact, I have one particular vehicle in mind that includes something extra. Is this something you may want to consider?"

Note that more likely than not, you will have enticed them to further engage by not only presenting a new curiosity, but by also not definitively answering their first question. When you feel that your customers are only mildly interested or have made lots of other inquires by the context of their message, a more vague approach may likely be more enticing. As you interact more, you will soon better sense how to proceed.

If they do not return your call, call them back again. Keep trying until you get a hold of them, sometimes varying your message with more or less encouragements. If you are unsuccessful after a while, it may be that they have lost interest or set an appointment elsewhere. If this is the case, you may have to try calling from another number to reinitiate their interest.

IN PERSON

When you reach the customer on the phone, simply follow the method of setting an appointment that we discussed in our phone chapter. Engage them, provide information, build rapport, and promise additional information when they visit. If you do reach them by phone, always follow up with an immediate email to reiterate your appointment time and personal information.

BY WAY OF EMAIL

If they don't leave their phone number or if you have received their voicemail, you will also want to send them an email of encouragement as well. An example of your message here will be very similar to the one you would leave on their answering machine. One may be, "Hi. Thank you for your interest in *xyz*. Please know that we have that and many similar vehicles available. Would it be convenient for you to come in this evening?"

Another may be, "Hi. Thank you for your inquiry. Would you be interested in the one with the chrome step bars or the one with a painted finish?" Again, adjust your message to the inquiry. In all cases, phone and email, you want to respond immediately and seek to entice a response in order to start a dialogue.

ALWAYS FOLLOW YOUR BEST PATH

The key point to understand when responding is that your customer's future moves will almost always be driven by their future wants. So make them want. I know that certain internet managers or sales managers may disagree with this philosophy when setting an appointment. They believe and will even teach you to believe that the web is sacred and should only be used for direct and fast information purposes. They will have you send the invoice, the availability, and even the bottom line price. However, this should be questioned. In the very early stages of the internet, when only information-oriented people used the net, this may have been more understandable. But now, the web is such a regular part of everyday life that almost everyone uses it in some fashion. Normal, everyday people are now the majority of users, and so I believe, that normal everyday rules should apply. Introduce yourself, build credibility and rapport with the sharing of certain information, and then further create their interest to visit by offering more for when they do.

THE CURIOUS WILL REMAIN

Have you ever noticed when someone reads a top ten list, he or she will always start with number ten and proceed to number one? Is it fair to build on someone's curiosity like this? Wouldn't it just be easier to know what number one was up front, so we could better decide when we would tune in or out?

Have you ever noticed how a game show host will always save announcing the winning answer until after the commercial? Is this fair? Is it fair that we will have to sit through the commercial to learn the result? Is it fair that we must pay for the show's airtime by watching its commercials? Well, fair or not, do we hang around to see who won?

Have you ever started reading a book or were thinking of seeing a movie and accidentally overheard the ending? Did your building desire and developing suspense continue with the same intensity? Did your curiosity compel you to stay interested? Did it?

If not, please know that this is the same for your customers. When you give your customers all of the requested information up front, they too will lose interest. Trust this. Do not squelch your potential customer's desire, instead, learn to kindle and further build their desire.

The whole process of sales both starts and finishes with the building and creating of additional motivation. Each step of the sales process is best ended with an enticement to move to the next. This is the secret to sales. This is how the whole process gets started and continues. In some transactions, this occurs accidentally, and in some transactions, it is a planned strategy. Please know that successful people will always have this as their plan, not just as a chance happening. Have you ever ventured further than you normally would just to uncover the whole truth? Have you ever been enticed into proceeding with the promise of additional information? Have you? Well, of course you have. This method of creating curiosity is both effective and common. It has also become accepted. The purpose of our process is to take our customers through the steps and toward the sale smoothly and efficiently. Build your customers desire to visit and then build their desire to own, and always believe that it's all in the steps.

DEVELOP YOUR CREATIVITY

The start of every contact should always be the same: examine your customer's inquiries, determine their key points of interest, and use them to develop the responses that will further peak their interest and compel them to respond.

The concept of this idea seems pretty simple to me, however, I have learned that where analysis and understanding come into play, there will always be different levels of acceptance and resulting abilities. Understanding your customer's interests and creating an effective response is going to take some thought. You will, without question, have to think before you respond. In the beginning, you will have to take the time to analyze your customer's inquiries to best determine their interests and your path. Having the creativity it takes to do this is not something you're going to learn from this or any other book. It is not random or simple knowledge. It's responsive to an action and must always reference that action. It is a combination of both creating and catering your question or response to encourage a response to a specific instance, thus it is impossible to list every best response for every action or inquiry.

257

To become better at creatively responding, try to think out certain interactions ahead of time. Set yourself up with some quiet time with no distractions and just think. Try to visualize the reactions each of your responses may have and then visualize the most effective. Put yourself in their position as you determine their motivations. Move back and forth from their position to yours and judge the reactions and effectiveness of each. Start with small visualizations of various scenarios and then further refine your abilities as you gather additional information that your future reactions create.

Our ability to be creative applies and relates to our success in this stage and in the total sales process as well. There is always a best time to be direct and respond directly, and there is also always a best time to respond in a manner that will further encourage a sale. To the experienced salesman, this is well understood and has probably become instinctive. However, many beginning salespeople, and ultimately unsuccessful salespeople, will never understand this. Many will start in this business and will never seem to understand the need for increasing one's desire. They will operate without the ability to encourage an interest and this will leave them without the positive experiences they will need to learn. Ultimately, they will set fewer appointments, sell fewer cars, and become further discouraged.

Well, if you are new, or if you feel you are headed down this path, stop. Change what you are doing. Quit trying to simply be a source of information and start contemplating how best to creatively entice your customers so they will want to move forward. I understand that it's easier and will take less thought to simply answer a customer's inquiries; however, to be successful you will sometimes have to prepare your path. Do not respond to their questions with direct and specific answers when that isn't what is best suited.

Although I'm sure it will take extra effort, practice, and experience to become effective. Please do not underestimate your ability to become creative. You don't have to be an experienced veteran to be successful here. I also do not believe that any one person is born more creative than another. I do feel, however, that some may be more easily conditioned or receptive in becoming successful simply as a result of their traits or habits. And, as we discussed earlier, your traits and habits can always be adjusted. So, if necessary, adjust some. Once you fully understand and set yourself to believe in this reasoning, and continue to learn and grow from your experiences, you can also believe that your abilities will only become stronger. Soon, your creatively constructed initial responses and instinctive follow-up responses will become natural, and your success will become imminent.

FINAL NOTE

Your only goal when communicating on the internet is to set an appointment. It is to take note of the customer's wants and needs, understand their motivations, look to increase them, and set the appointment. You have one goal, set the appointment. Set the appointment, set the appointment, set the appointment.

KEEPING YOUR FOCUS

The most successful salespeople in the automobile industry are those who believe in themselves, believe in their products, and believe in the quality of the service they offer. These qualities, when combined with a set sales process, are the building blocks of success. With these principals, your career will be one of achievement and reward.

The importance of keeping these qualities present and intact are essential in maintaining your positive outlook and preserving your future success. Sometimes the most difficult challenge in sales is keeping your focus and not letting surrounding factors limit your abilities. Keeping this focus is looking at the big picture. It is creating and confirming your beliefs to help stabilize your focus through all of the fluctuations that you experience. It is not letting anything or anyone influence you in a negative way.

When you are up, it is easy to keep going. It is when you are down and can pick yourself up that you are truly on your way to becoming successful. To help establish and further create your success, take the time to set yourself up with your own set of personal beliefs and commit yourself to them. Establish the beneficial philosophies that you trust and use them for guidance and support. Whenever things are not going quite right or you feel stuck in a negative situation, concentrate on your beliefs.

Many companies, in their efforts to be more successful in a competitive environment, have set themselves up with a "mission statement." A mission statement is an employee sanctioned doctrine of the commitment and dedication that they will be the best they can be. It is a writ of uncompromising allegiance to follow and believe in the philosophies and processes that will help them excel in their particular field. It provides the plan, the structure, and the goals to live by and forever improve upon.

I like such a statement, and believe that both its creation and its following will help any size company achieve higher highs, even one-person companies such as yourself. Your beliefs will help provide a source of determination that will give you the strength to remain successful through the challenges you will face.

THE PATH FOR SUCCESS

Here are some of the essentials that are the foundation to a successful career in the sales profession.

BELIEVE IN THE PROCESS

An assembly line is a system in which each step of the process has to be followed, one where each part of the process cannot be started until the previous step has been completed. The engine cannot be installed until the frame has been built. It is a process where there is no skipping of the steps, and where each step builds off the previous one.

This is the same with selling a car. Salespeople who are intent on becoming successful will have some type of a system that they follow. They will have a guide that helps guide them through the process of the sale. Their system will be one of forward progression and consistency.

Our process is a set of steps and guidelines that are ultimately designed to lead us on the proper path. It is a step-by-step process that will help us guide our customers from introduction to delivery. It, too, is a process in which each step relies on another and each step is essential to the sale. Any following step can only be achieved by completion of the preceding step. You build the rapport, to ask the questions, to gain the knowledge and credibility, to find a solution, and influence a purchase.

262

If you know that you will have to handle certain objections down the road, you'll be more likely to allow your process to acquire your credibility in the early stages. If you know there will come a time when you'll be presenting figures, you'll allow your process to build value throughout the preceding interaction. The attributes that makes our process so invaluable is its effectiveness and consistency. With the process, allow each step to be a new rung in your ladder. The best way to eat an apple is one bite at a time and this is the same for selling an automobile. Prepare yourself by practicing and rehearsing the steps in your process until they become second nature. This will help you better understand where you are with each step and how you can best get to the next. Having and following a process will help keep you focused on your results. Visualize your sale, and you will better understand your path.

The sales process has become habit to the top salesperson. Salespeople, who are prepared with the proper skills, have set plans to follow, and who are fluid in their delivery are sure to be successful in their careers.

BELIEVE IN YOURSELF

Believing in yourself is how you radiate confidence, and confidence is a necessary trait for someone who hopes to be persuasive. In sales, if you do not portray a credible belief in yourself, your customers will also have a hard time believing in you or your advice.

Belief in one's self starts from the inside. The true projection of yourself is not what you do or say, but what you are. It is what you believe in and what you have faith in. It is the result of your principles and values. You cannot build trust without honesty, and you cannot project trust without self-belief. These traits will only shine through when they come from within. Please understand this and seek to adjust your internal approach if necessary. One who lacks the depth of these will be transparent to others. People will be much more likely to see you for who you are than for whom you pretend to be, so find strength in yourself.

To help yourself in this area, take the time to measure where your confidence level presently is and then determine how best to increase it if necessary. Learn to recognize and understand the importance of the earlier chapter, where we talked about the beneficial traits of a salesperson, and become aware of where you may need some improvement. Assess and then realign yourself with the traits and habits that will help give you your strength, and then allow yourself to grow, improving your qualities as you proceed. Once you build your foundation with good qualities and solidify them in your actions, yourself belief will be more likely to shine and your results will likely be successful. Know that as you begin to add to and adjust your traits, you will become stronger and will soon have more belief in yourself.

Achieving a successful sales career is much like building a relationship. We grow and obtain success by building successful relationships with our dealership, our fellow employees, and our customers. In sales, business, and in life, know your relationships will always be more likely to excel if you establish yourself as a person who truly believes in him or herself.

BELIEVE IN YOUR PRODUCT

Believe in the product you sell and the service you provide. Until you can convince your customers that you truly believe in your automobile line, you will not be totally effective in convincing them to purchase.

First and most importantly, choose an automobile line that you like. This seems to make sense, but it is surprising how many salespeople are selling a vehicle line they do not believe in. They feel that their technique is enough to satisfy their income. Well, they are fooling themselves. This is crazy. If this is true of you, stop. You will never meet your top potential unless you believe in the product you are selling. If you believe in Hondas, sell Hondas. If you believe in

Fords, sell Fords. There are tens of thousands of dealerships in the world and each area has a host of different ones.

Choose a vehicle line and dealership that is right for you. Then continue to learn and study your vehicles and your competition's vehicles as well. Discover and understand all of the benefits and shortcomings of each and become relentless in your pursuit to understand how each will line up with the customers you meet. Become dedicated to knowing, understanding, and recognizing the features and benefits of all your vehicles. Understand that when you can truly realize and appreciate the benefits of your vehicles and dealership, you will be better at helping others appreciate them, too.

STRIVE FOR EXCELLENCE

If this is the profession you have chosen, you owe it to yourself, your customers, and your dealership to perform at a high level. Commit yourself to perform to the best of your ability.

CONTINUE TO TRAIN AND SELF EDUCATE

The best salespeople are constantly seeking to educate themselves. Great salespeople are not born; they study and learn their trade. One of the top traits that successful salespeople share is their ability and desire to learn. I think the expression, "a natural-born salesperson," came about because some salespeople are so studied and practiced that it appears they must have been born with, "it." However, they were not. Different actions provoke different responses from different people. Understanding this is not innate, it is a product of training and experience. Always believe in your ability to better yourself. A true achiever is never done learning.

Seek to expand your learning from within and outside your profession. The more diverse your learning program is, the better you will become in your field. The differences in people are as multiple and complex as the differences in products. Studying a diverse background of products and intended clients is beneficial because it helps develop your ability to adapt to the people you will meet. Just because you are selling the same product over and over does not mean you are selling the same people. In addition to your dealership's training, take the time to watch other salespeople in their places of business. Appliance stores, jewelry stores, clothing boutiques, and furniture stores are but a few that have commissioned salespeople. Find out who the top salesperson is at each location and listen to what they say and do. Learn from others. Use every source you can. Watch the attorneys on TV, listen to the carnival stand operators, and hang out in furniture showrooms. Pay attention to their actions.

Sometimes it's just as important to learn what not to do as it is to learn what you should do. Study what works for other salespeople, and learn from their mistakes. Take note of their introductions and follow their interactions. Look for their process and analyze it. Learn from where they may have done better and from where they may have succeeded. Take note of their customer's language, actions, and responses. Learn how to better read and understand people, and how to better succeed by comparing the similarities and differences with your own sales process. Be excited the next time the phone rings and it is a sales call. Stay up one night for the late night infomercial. Spend quality time in the malls and shopping centers. Seriously, take advantage of all the learning opportunities available and continue to increase your knowledge and understanding.

Learning is everything. It is how you obtain the knowledge that is essential to succeed. It is investing in yourself and your future. This investment is the essence of this book. Build your foundation in your career and seek to build upon it. Now that you have finished reading this book, keep it and use it as a reference for a successful career. Make a commitment to yourself to be successful.

Good luck.

NOW AVAILABLE
THE AUDIO VERSION

Made in the USA
San Bernardino, CA
26 July 2018